East End Photos
Through Mayar's Eyes
Photo Album: Tower Hamlets, Random, One

Mayar Akash

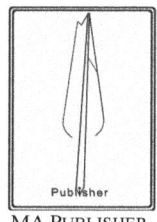

MA PUBLISHER

Copyright © Mayar Akash 2020

Published by MA Publishing (Penzance)
Published October 2020
ISBN-13: 978-1-910499-58-0

All rights reserved. No part of this publication may be reproduced, stored in a retrieval system, or transmitted, in any form or by any means, electronic, mechanical, photocopying, recording, public performances or otherwise, without prior written permission of the copyright holder, except for brief quotations embodied in critical articles or reviews.

Cover designed by Mayar Akash
Typeset in Times New Roman
All photos belong to Mayar Akash

 Paper printed on is FSC Certified, lead free, acid free, buffered paper made from wood-based pulp. Our paper meets the ISO 9706 standard for permanent paper. As such, paper will last several hundred years when stored.

Introduction

This is a first in the a series photo books featuring the photographs I've taken over the years growing up in the East End of London. When I first got my first camera in the late 80's, I started snapping away Today I present those photos captured through Mayar's Eyes, as I grew and my curiosity and ideas changed and formed.

The environment changed along with the people and social issues, they all had a bearing on my world.

For many years I didn't know what to do with them but now it seem fit to organise them like an albums and publish them, give access to the world, to see the East End through a Bangladeshi, Sylheti living in Tower Hamlets, with the urban factor; no hold bars assimilation into the Cockney East End, perspective.

The photos are not in any particular order, they are all random, I want to give people a taster of random things that I have encounter in my life journey.

I have ensured that all images as clearly marked with the date and the time stamp, and for some images brief description to assist, however, generally just date and time. The images are random and peruser's interpretations will be subjective, and that is how I feel is best left.

"Date & Time stamped photos, I know where I was, do you know where you were in the world?"

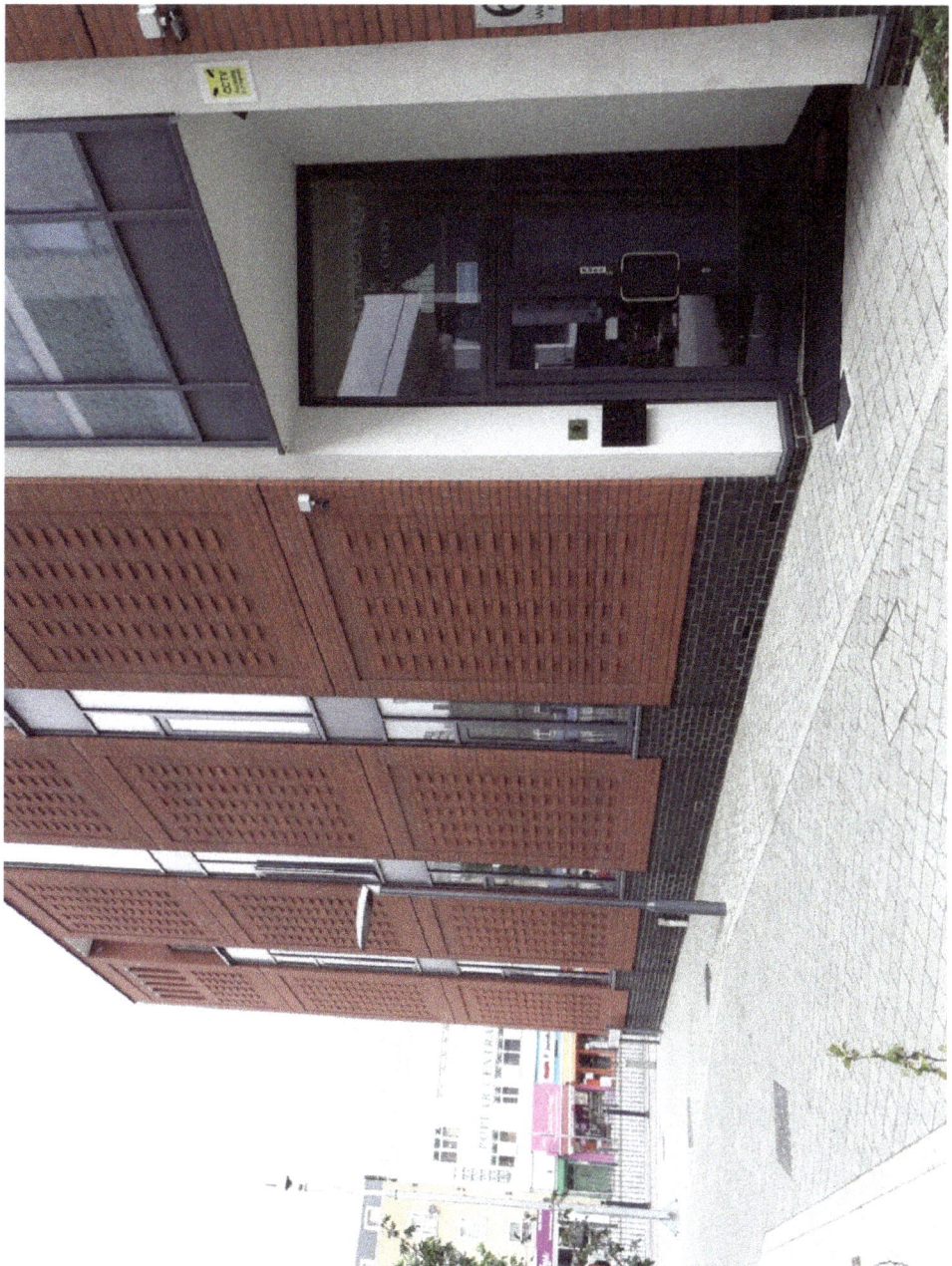

11.9.2017: - 12:23, Webber Street Mosque Building, Webber Street, Poplar

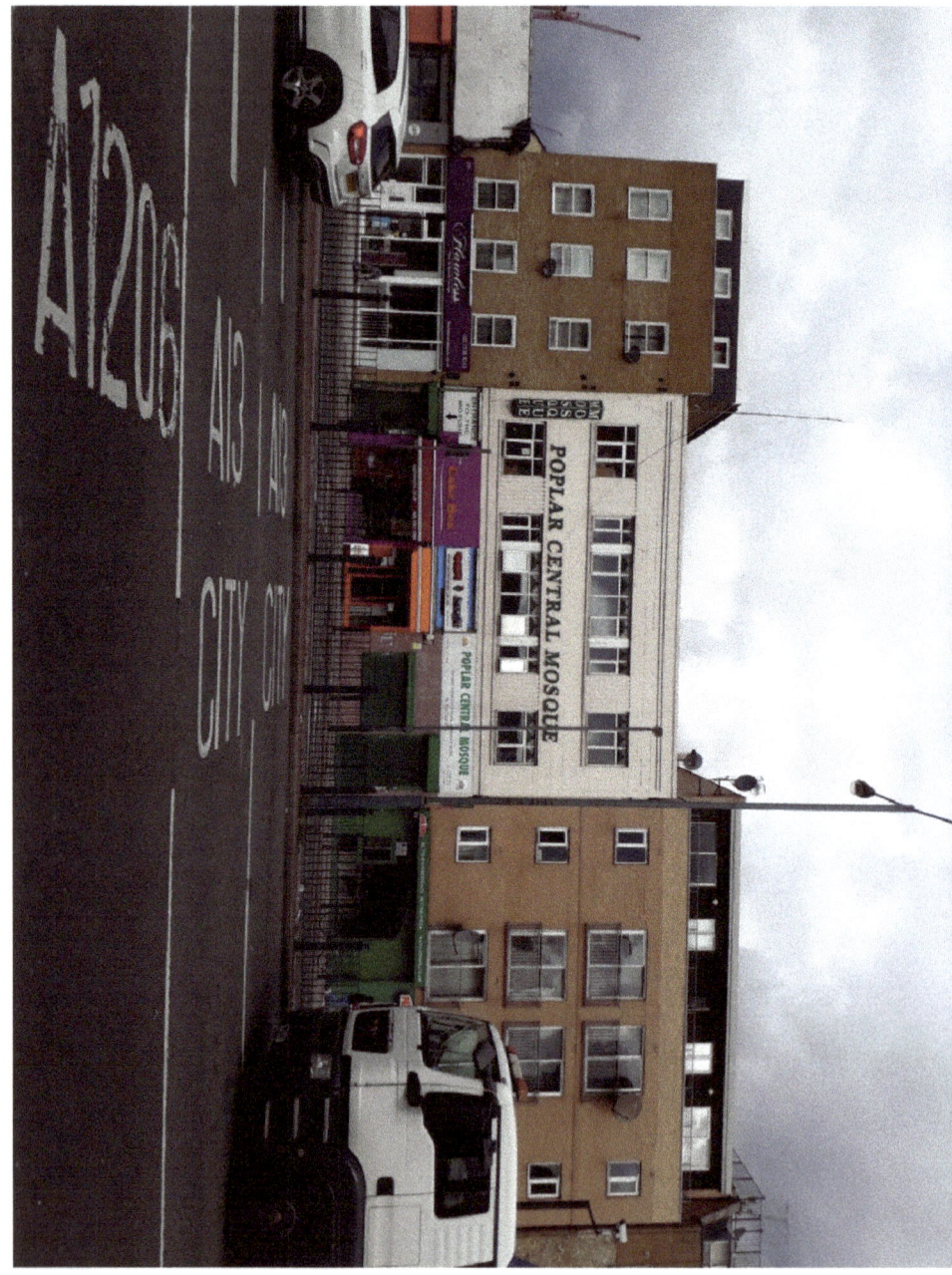

11.9.2017 - 12;24, Poplar Central Mosque on East India Dock Road.

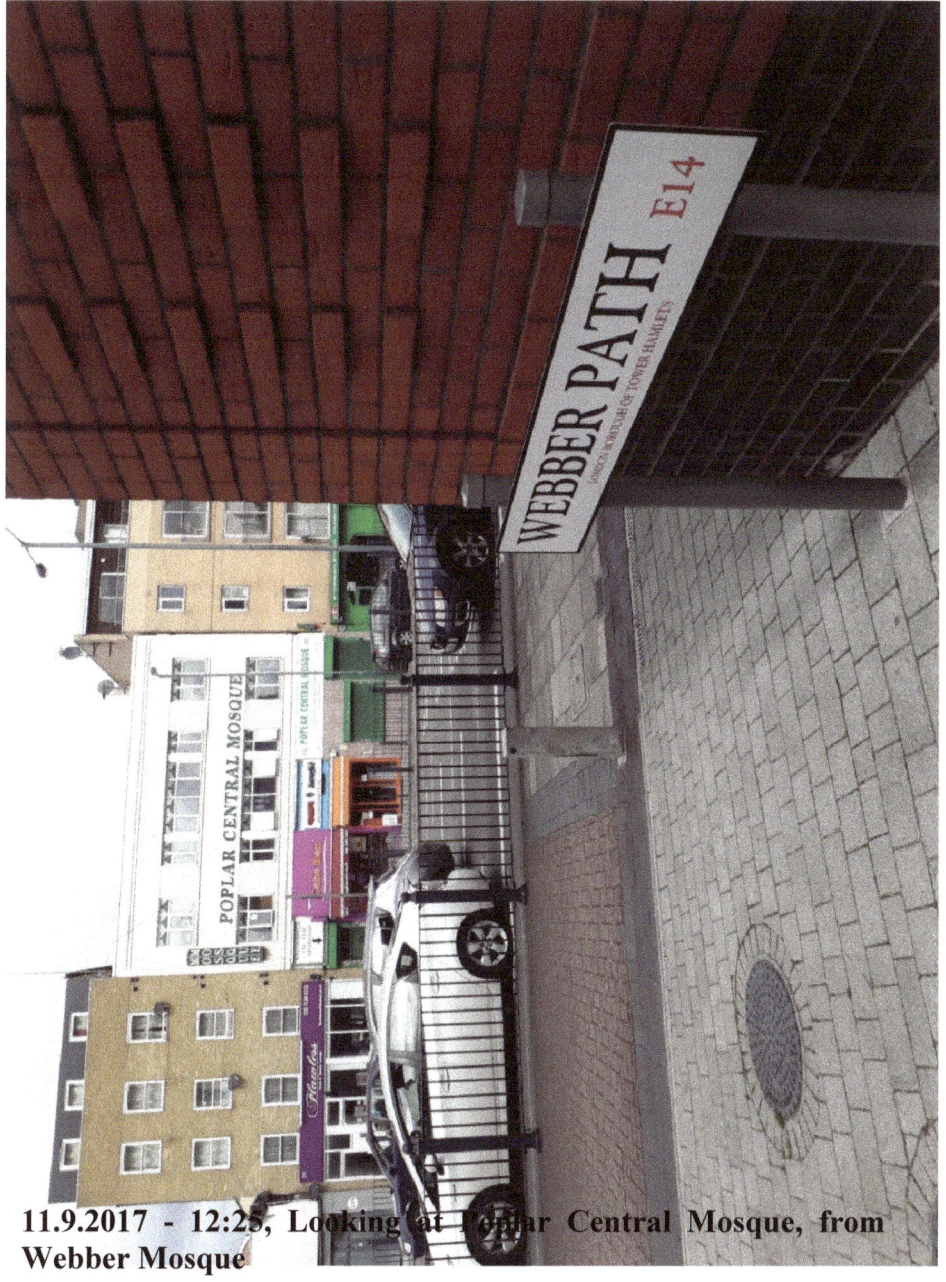

11.9.2017 - 12:25, Looking at Poplar Central Mosque, from Webber Mosque

Distance from one mosque to another, a stones throw away.

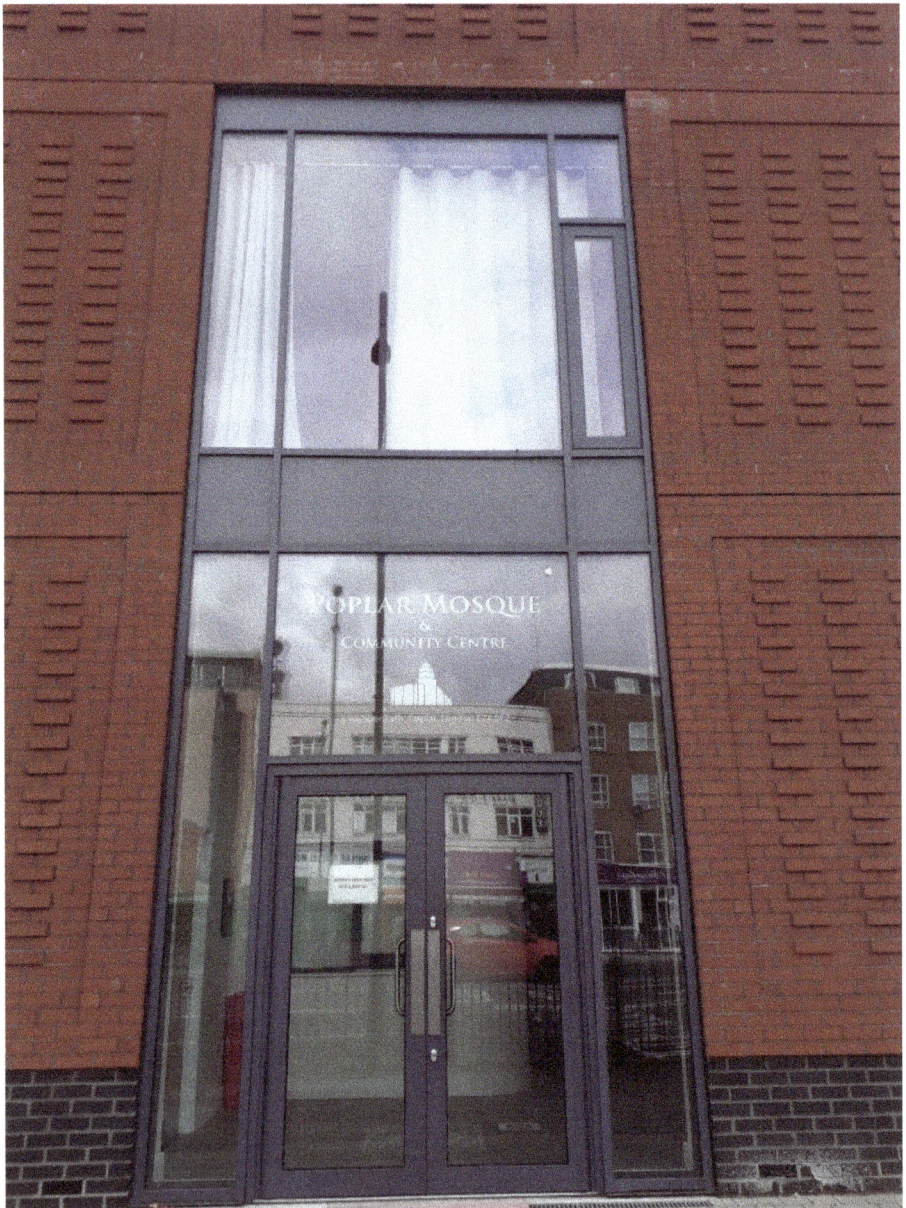

11.9.2017 - 12:24:51, Mosque entrance

I was capturing the state of affairs of the residents in the borough, village dogma, a mosque in every village.

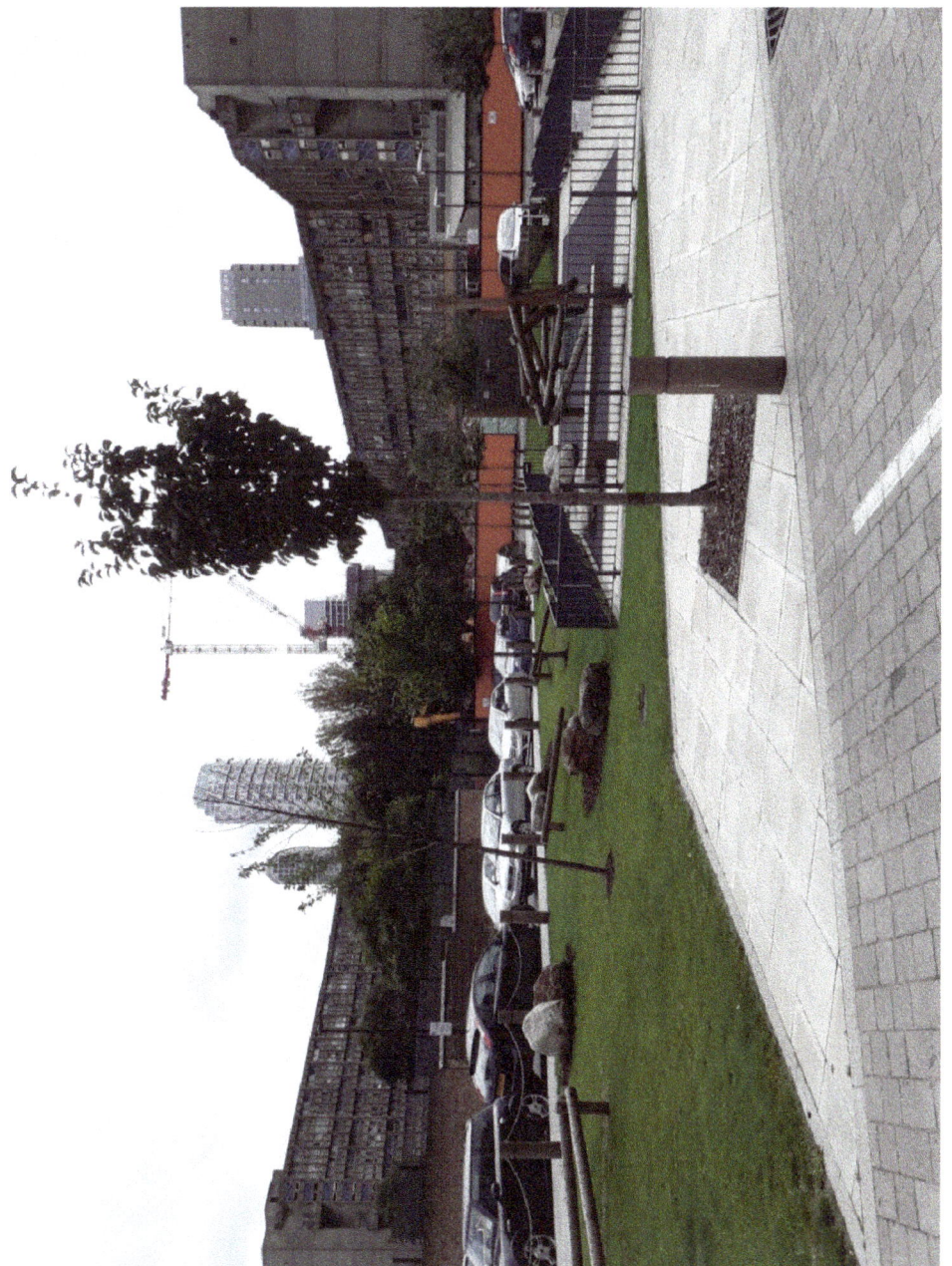

11.9.2017:-12:26:53, Webber Mosque Landscaping, looking towards Robinhood Gardens

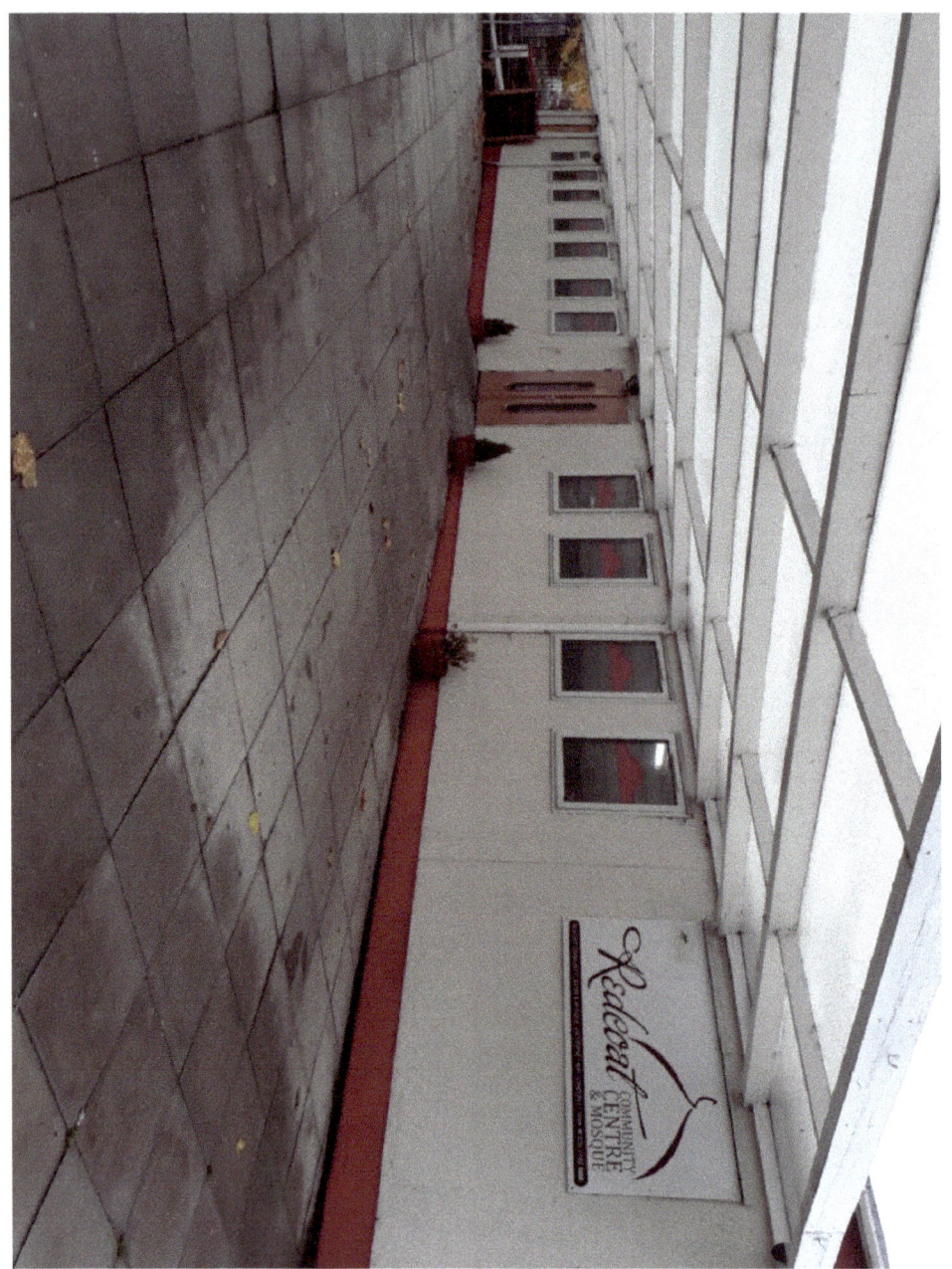

11.11.2017 - 10:59:04, Redcoat Mosque, Stepney Way.

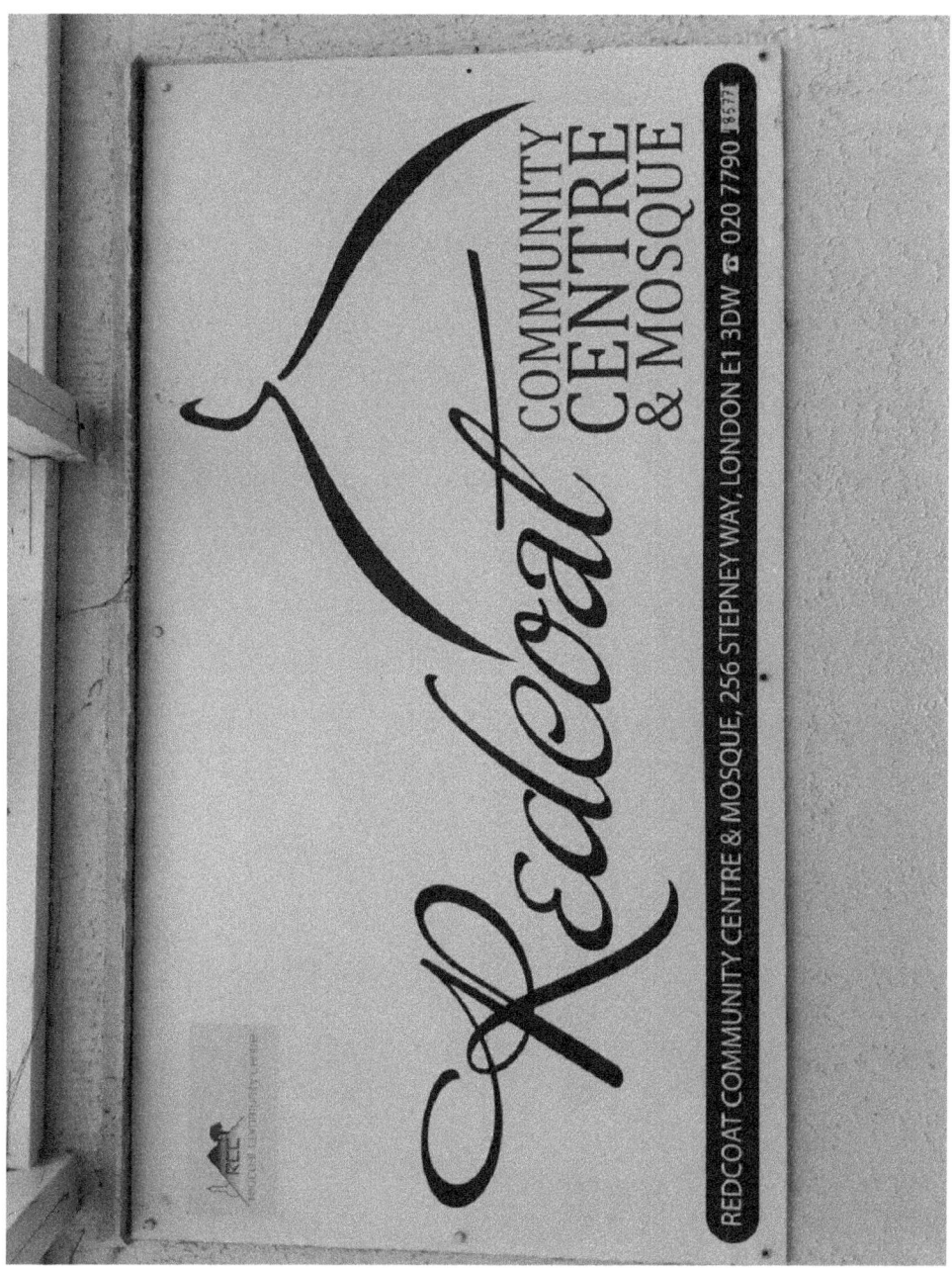

11.11.2017 - 10:59:42, Redcoat Mosque, Stepney Way

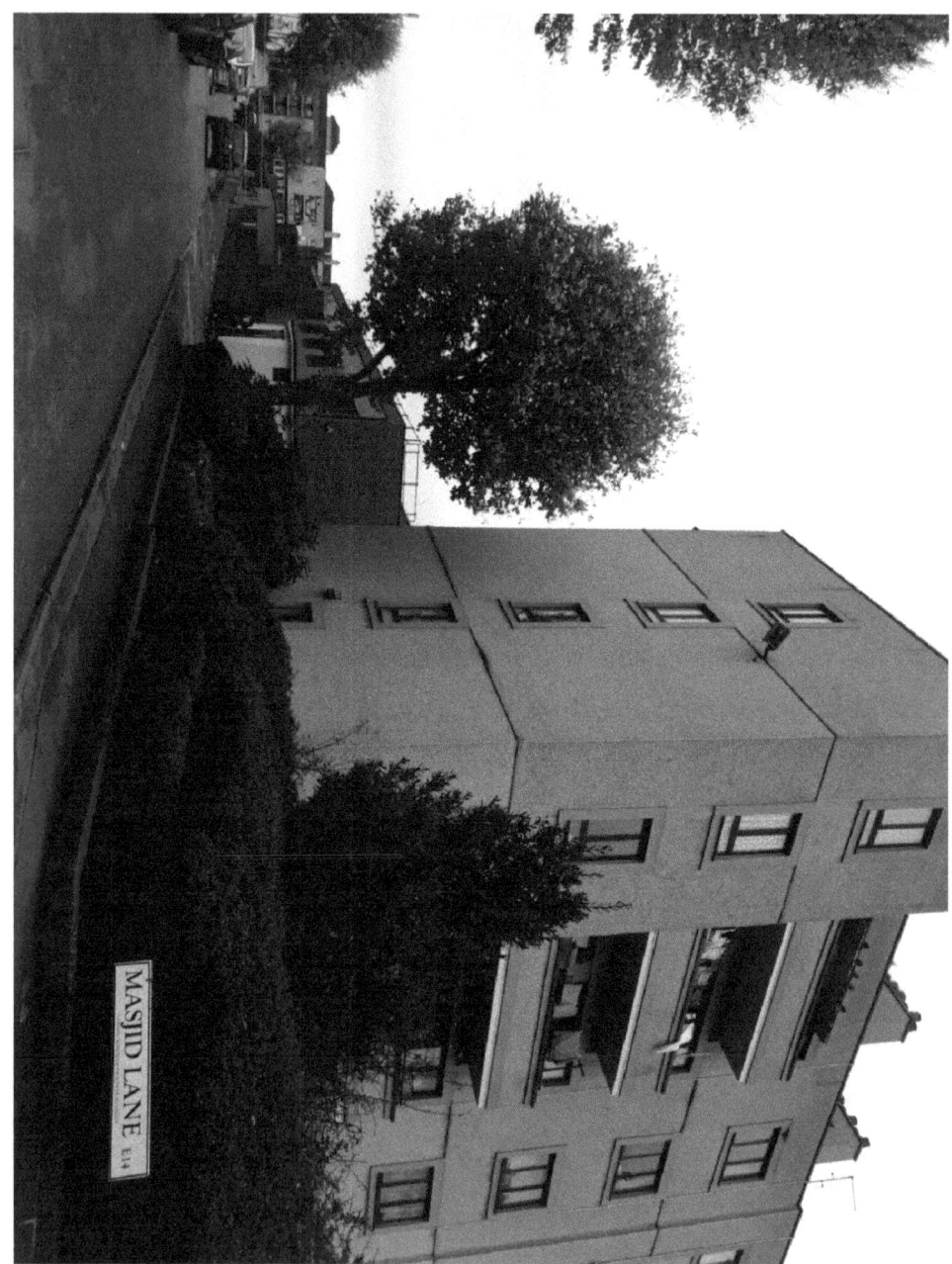

21.11.2017 - 12:54:46, Burdett estate,

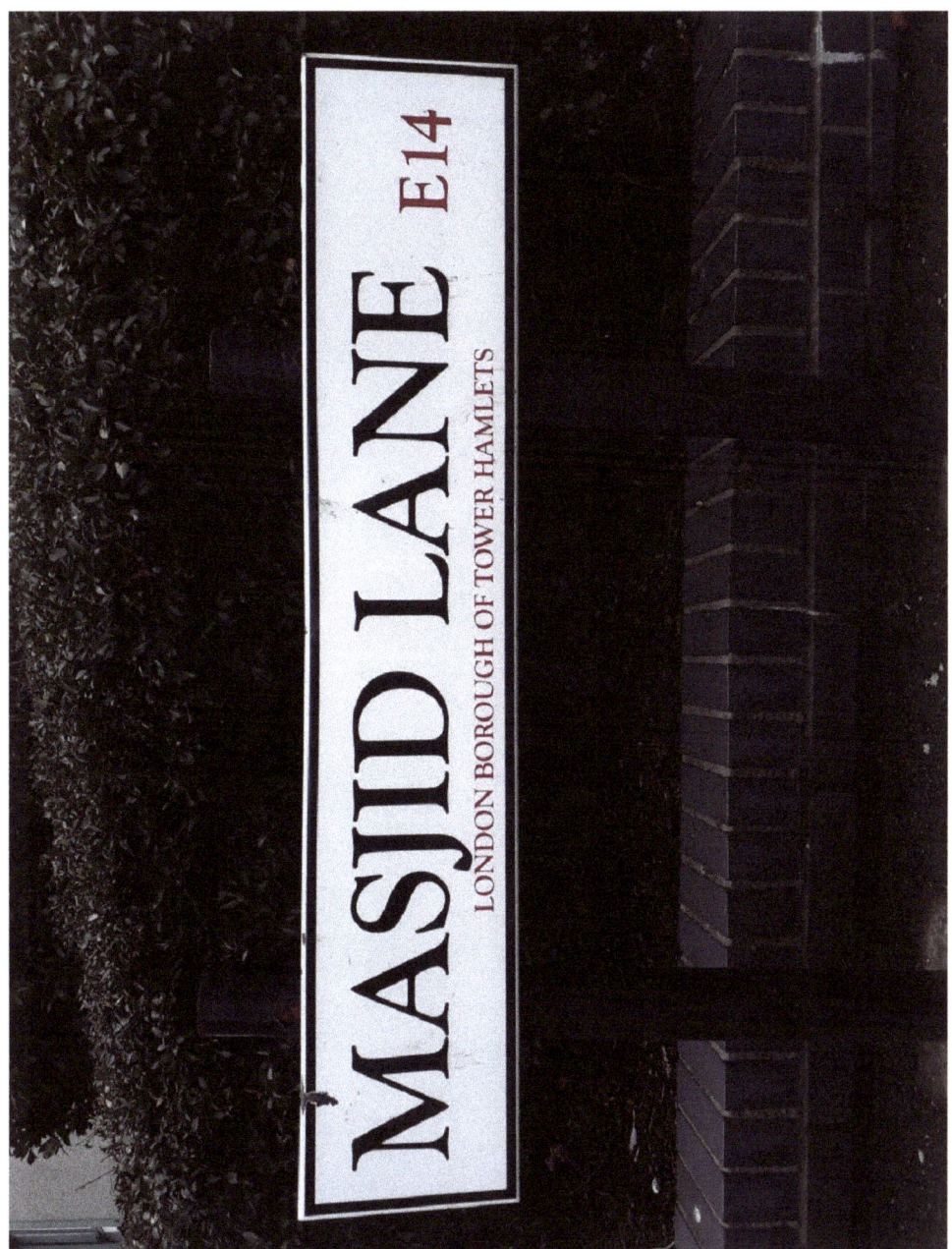

20.11.2017 - 12:54:20, Burdett Estate

I must say this mosque was intelligently planned out.

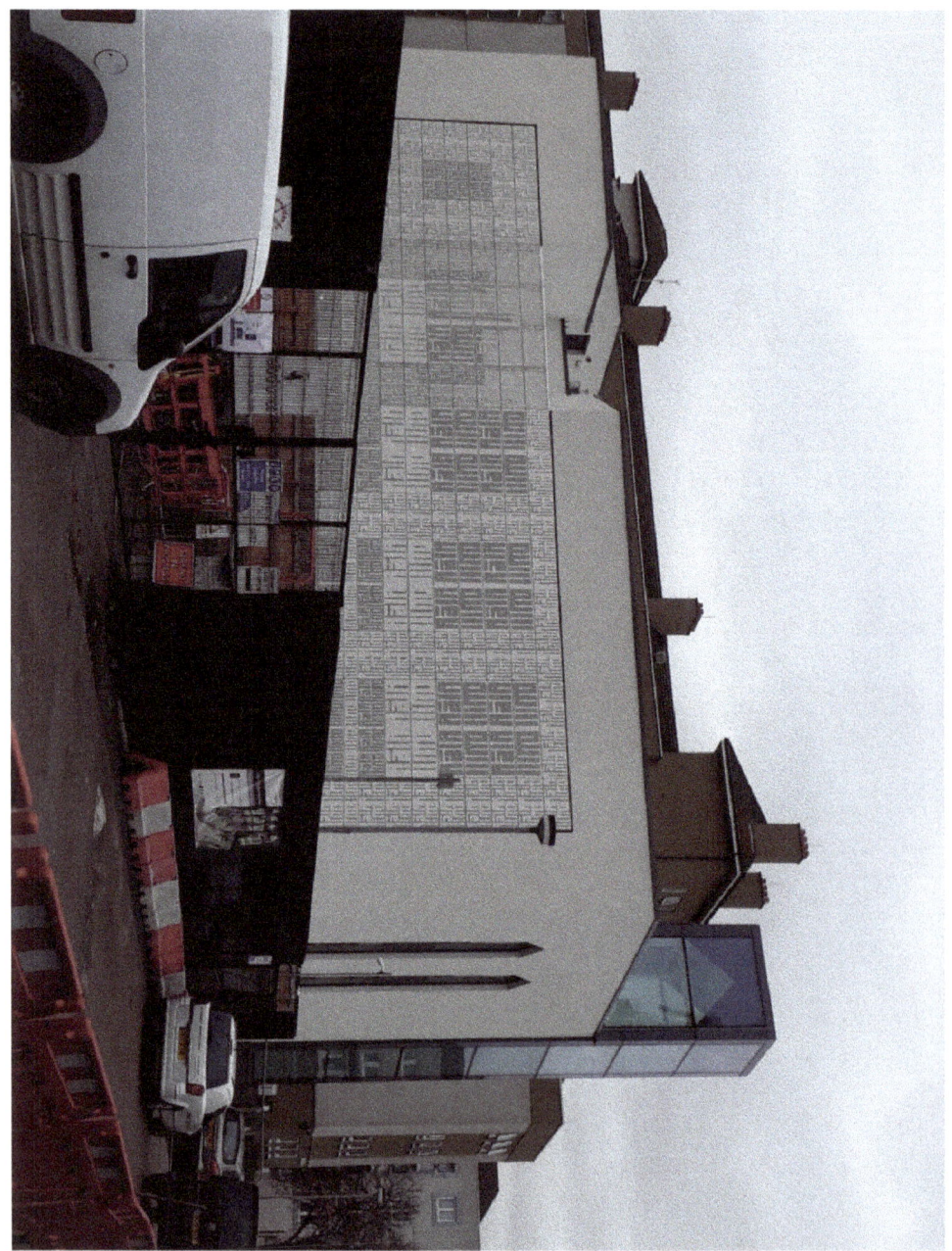

20.11.2017 - 12:56:11, Burdett Estate Mosque Development

The minaret, incorporated as a section of the building, is great!

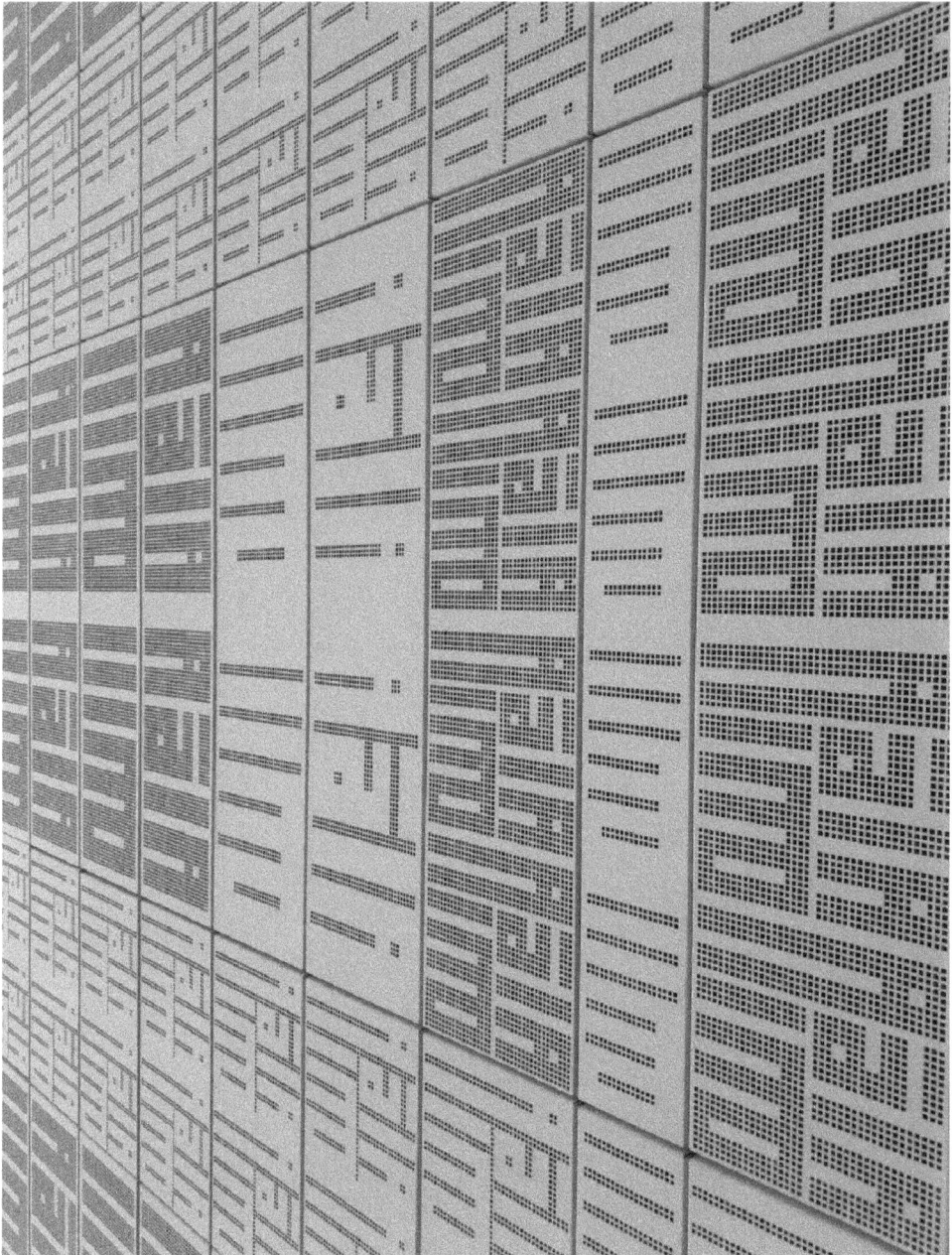

20.11.2017 - 12:58:26, Burdett Estate Mosque

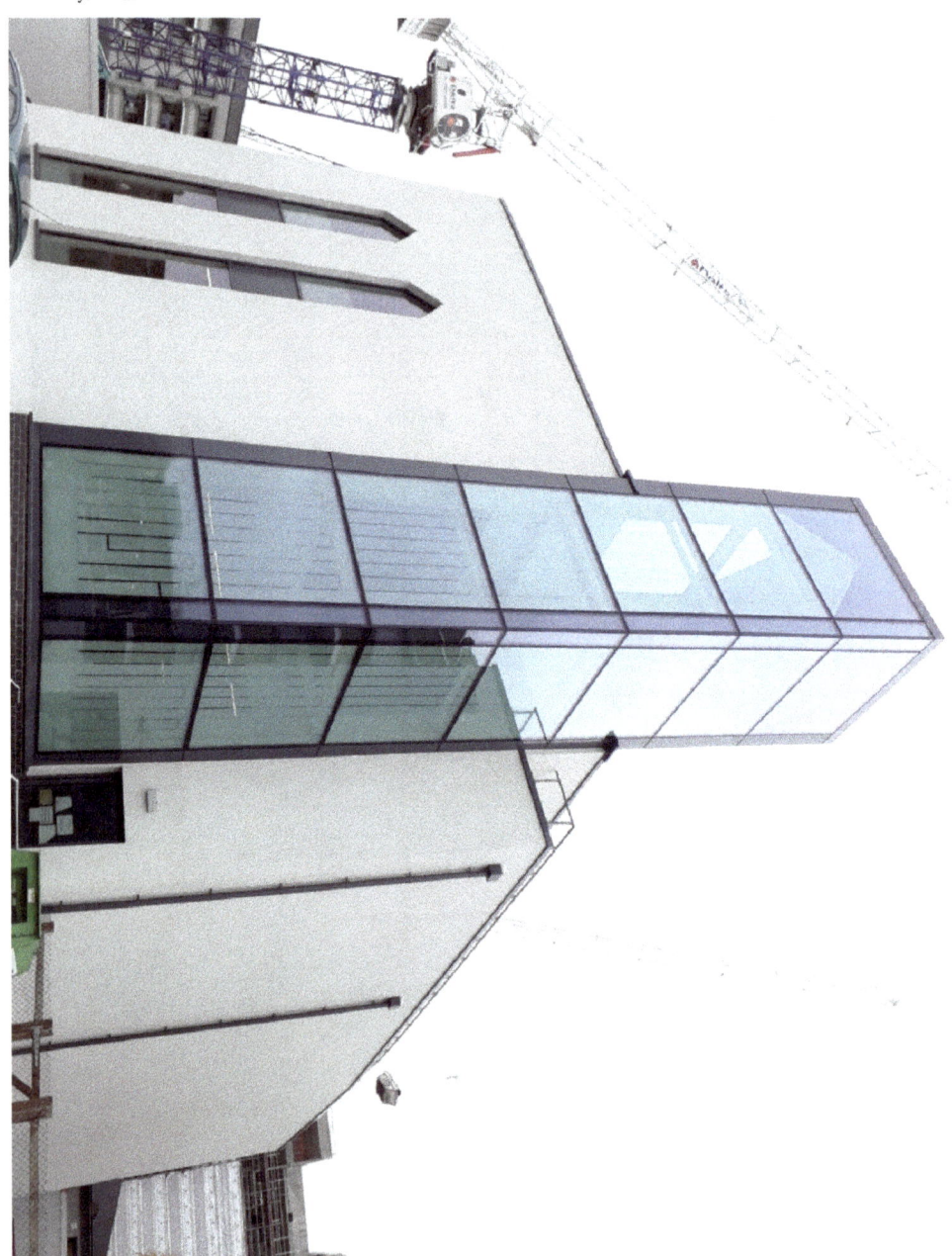

20.11.2017 -12:57:05, Burdett Estate Mosque with glass Mineret

East End Photos, Through Mayar's Eyes : **Tower Hamlets, Random One**

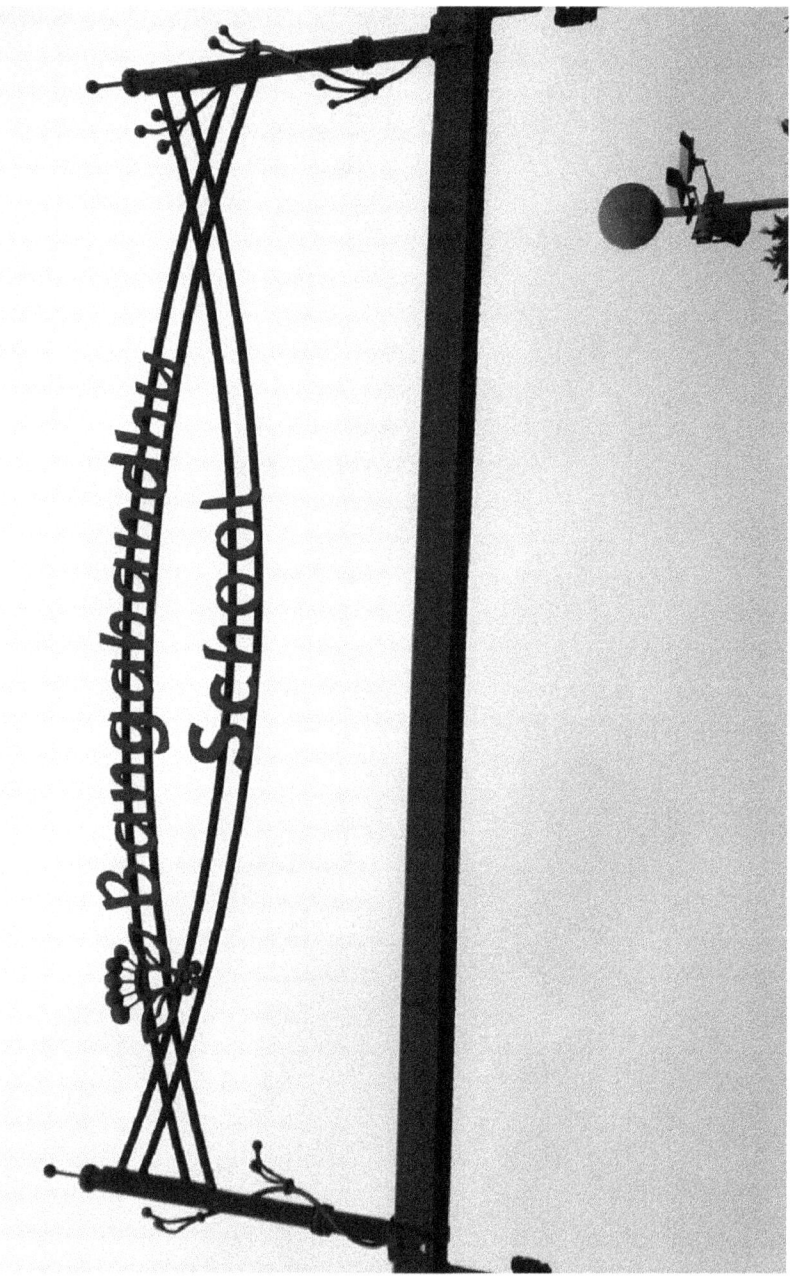

20.11.2017 - 13:13:25, Bangabandu School Sign, Wessex Street

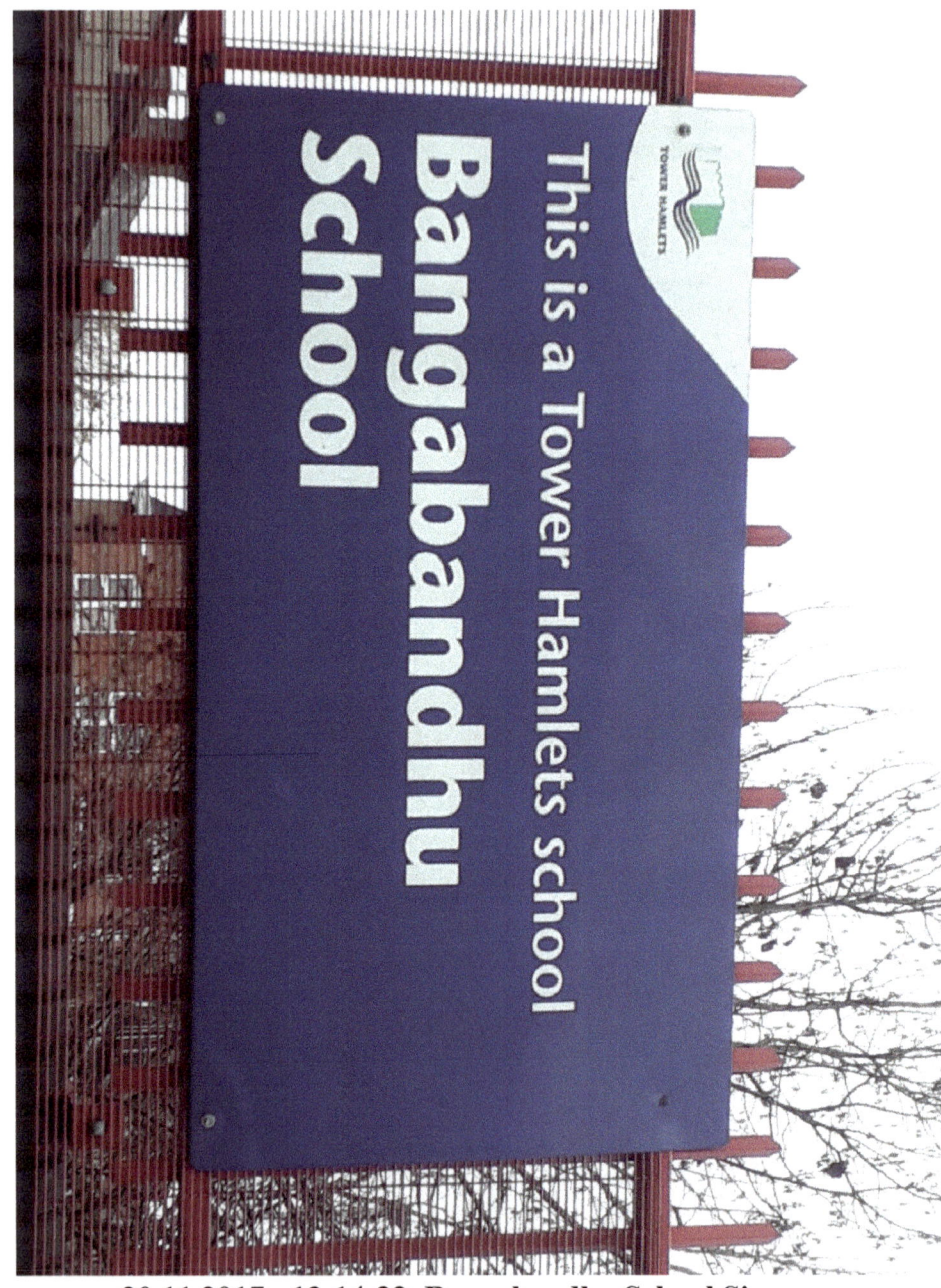

20.11.2017 - 13:14:22, Bangabandhu School Sign

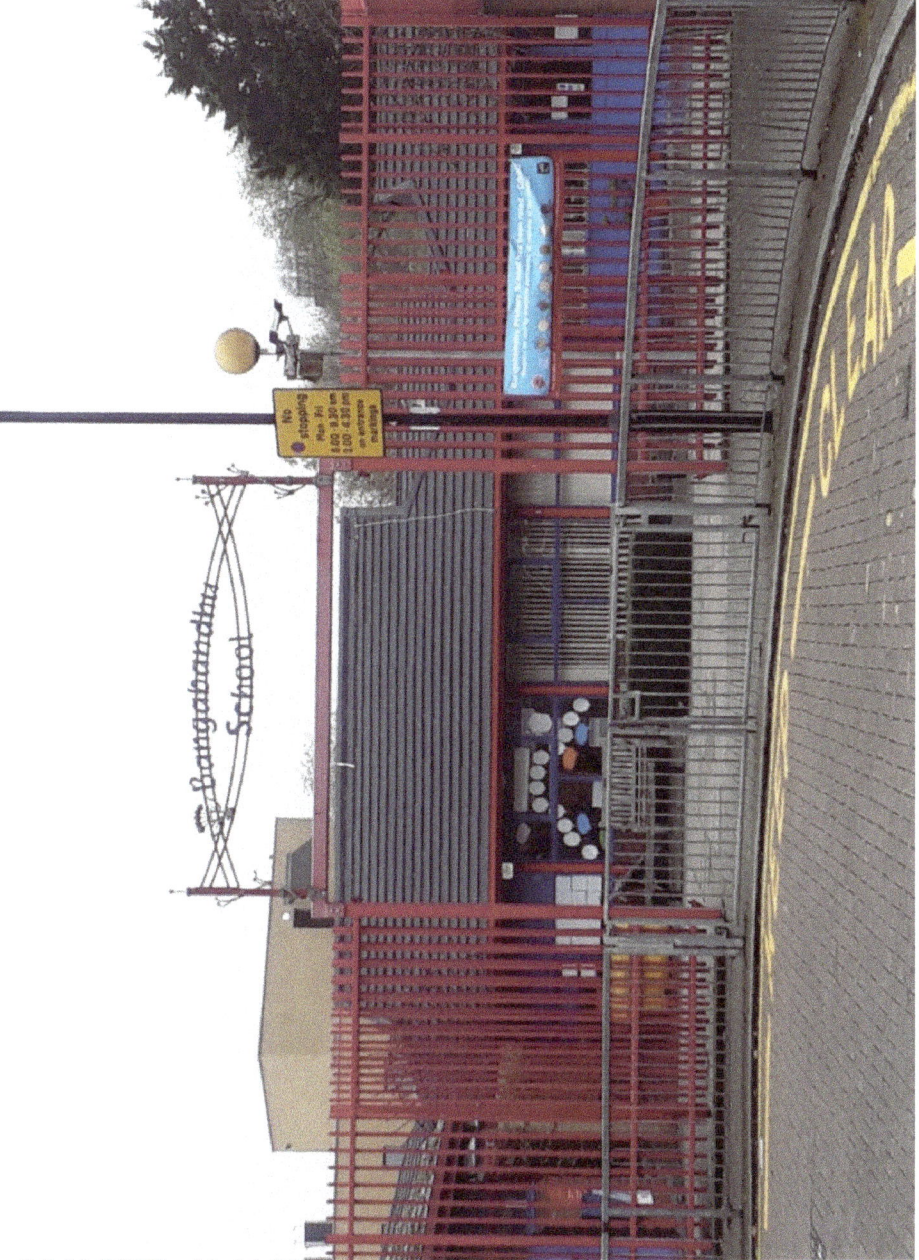

20.11.2017 - 13:14:22, Bangabandhu School, Wessex Street.

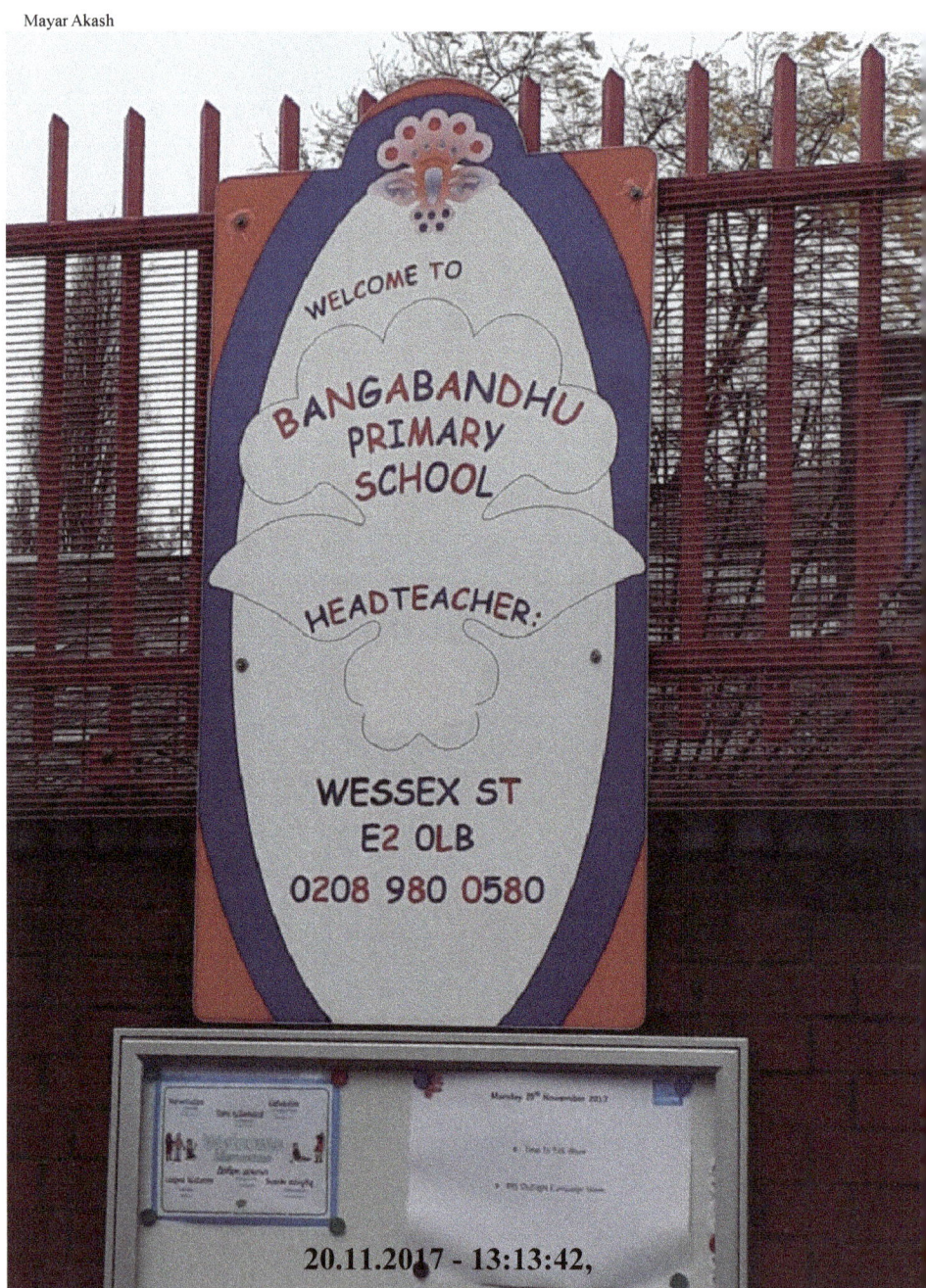

20.11.2017 - 13:13:42,

This school was built in the height of the Bangladeshi Communities accomplishments in the Borough of Tower Hamlets, through the pursuit via the Local political due processes.

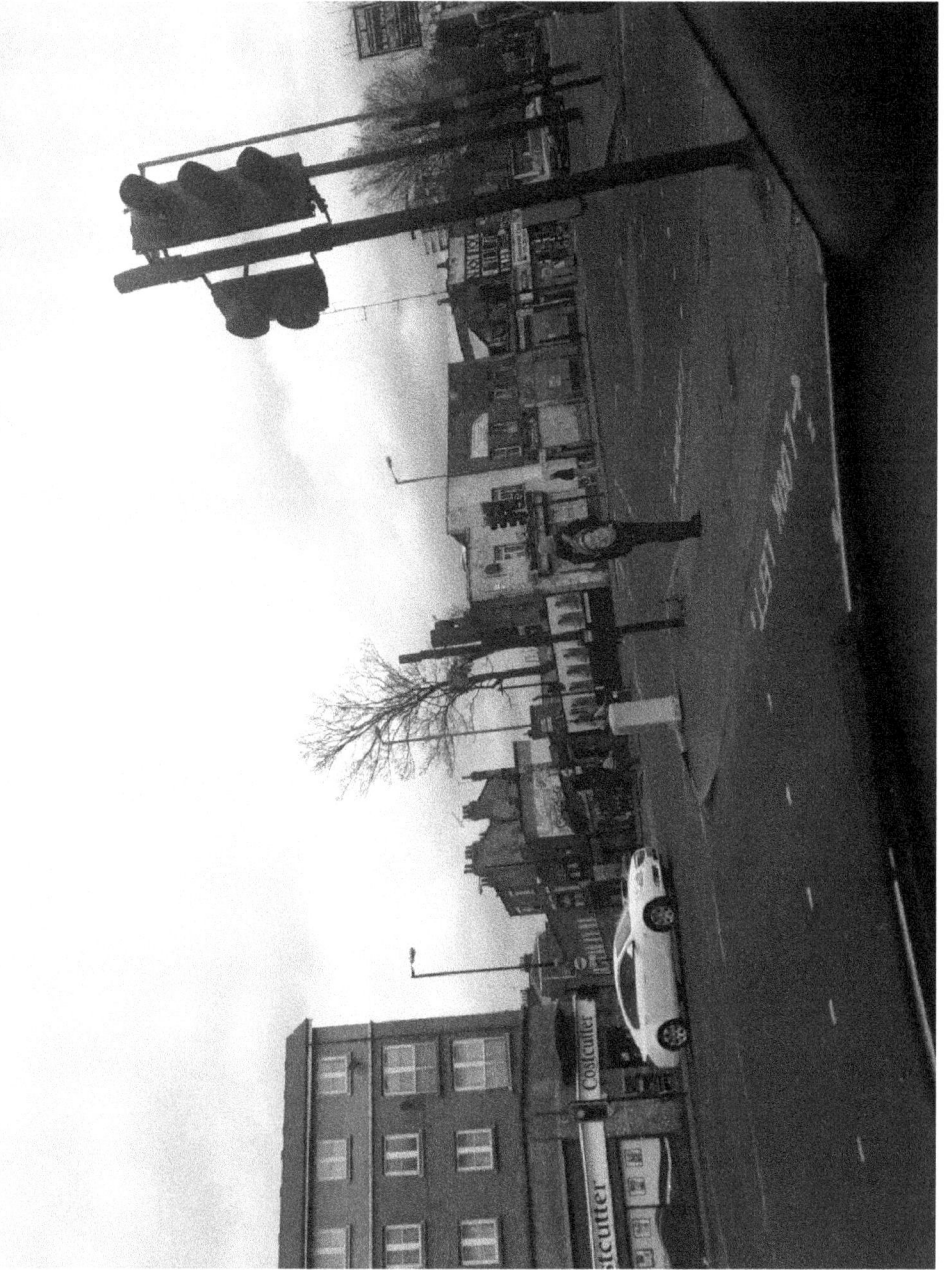

04.04.2018 - 13:53:29, Commercial Road Junction with Limehouse Link approach road

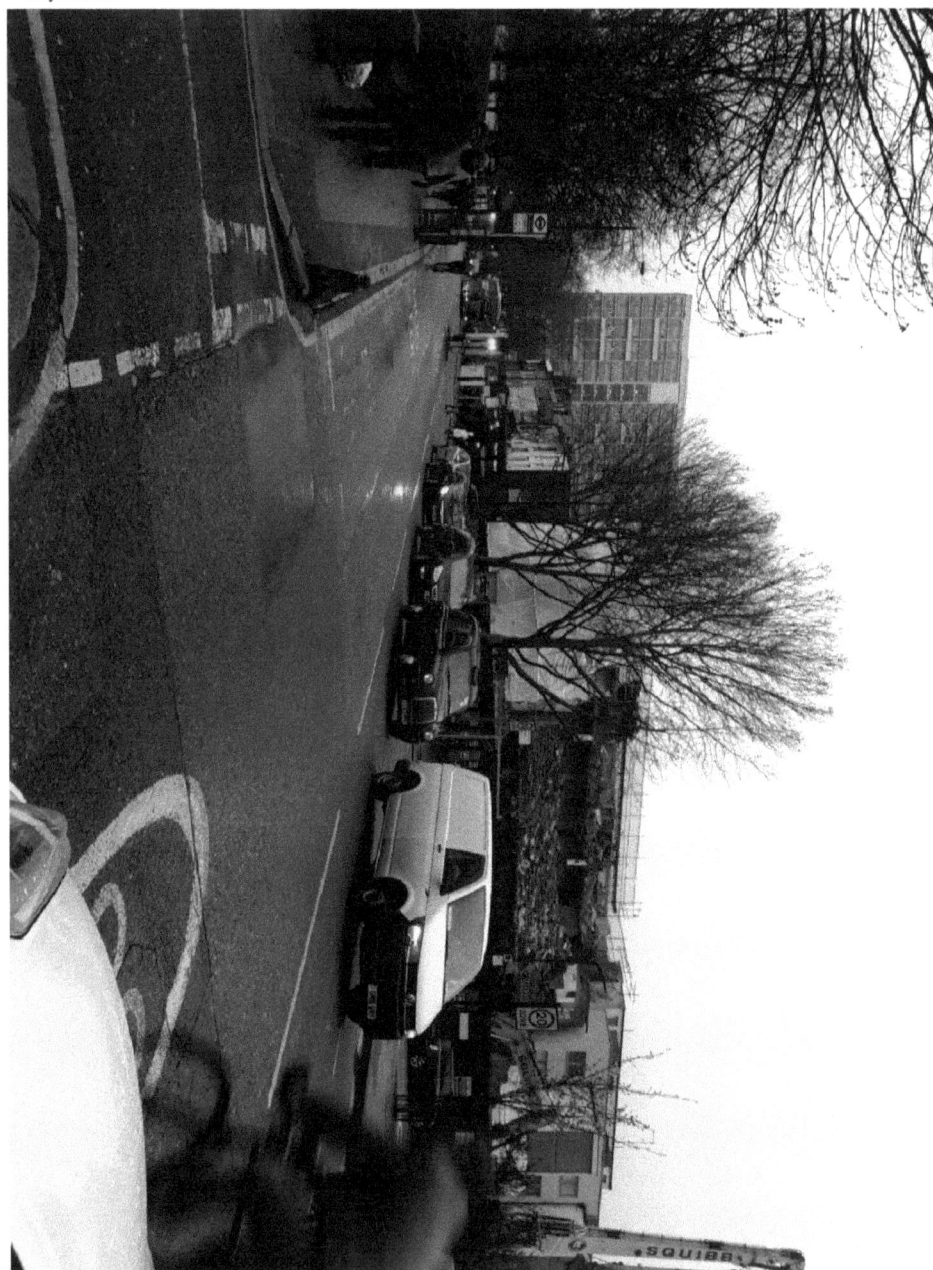

09.04.2018 - 18:41:55, Hackney Road, Demolition of the Bingo hall

East End Photos, Through Mayar's Eyes : **Tower Hamlets, Random One**

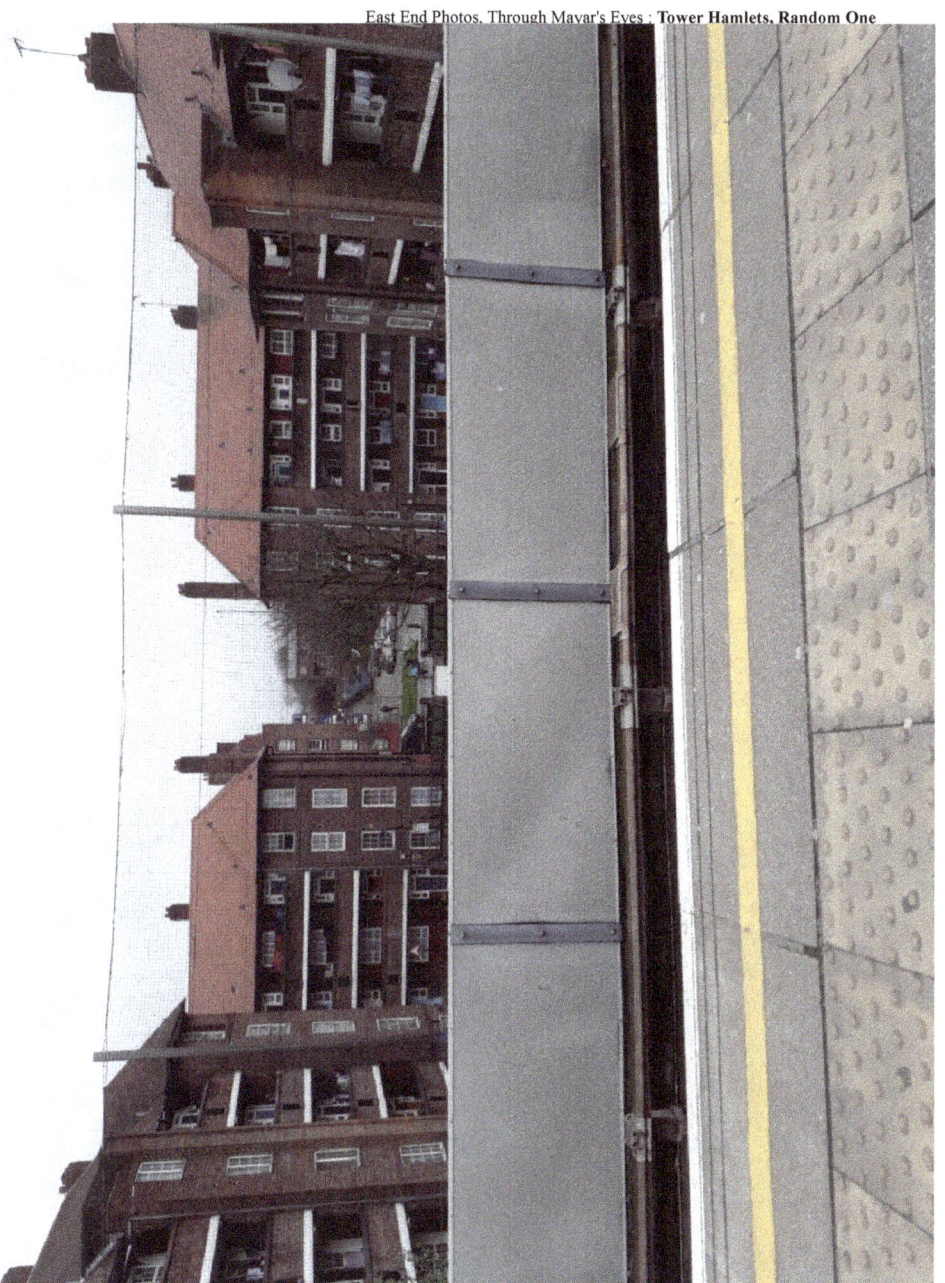

13.4.2018 - 14:38:31, View of Shadwell Gardens Estate from Shadwell DLR Platform

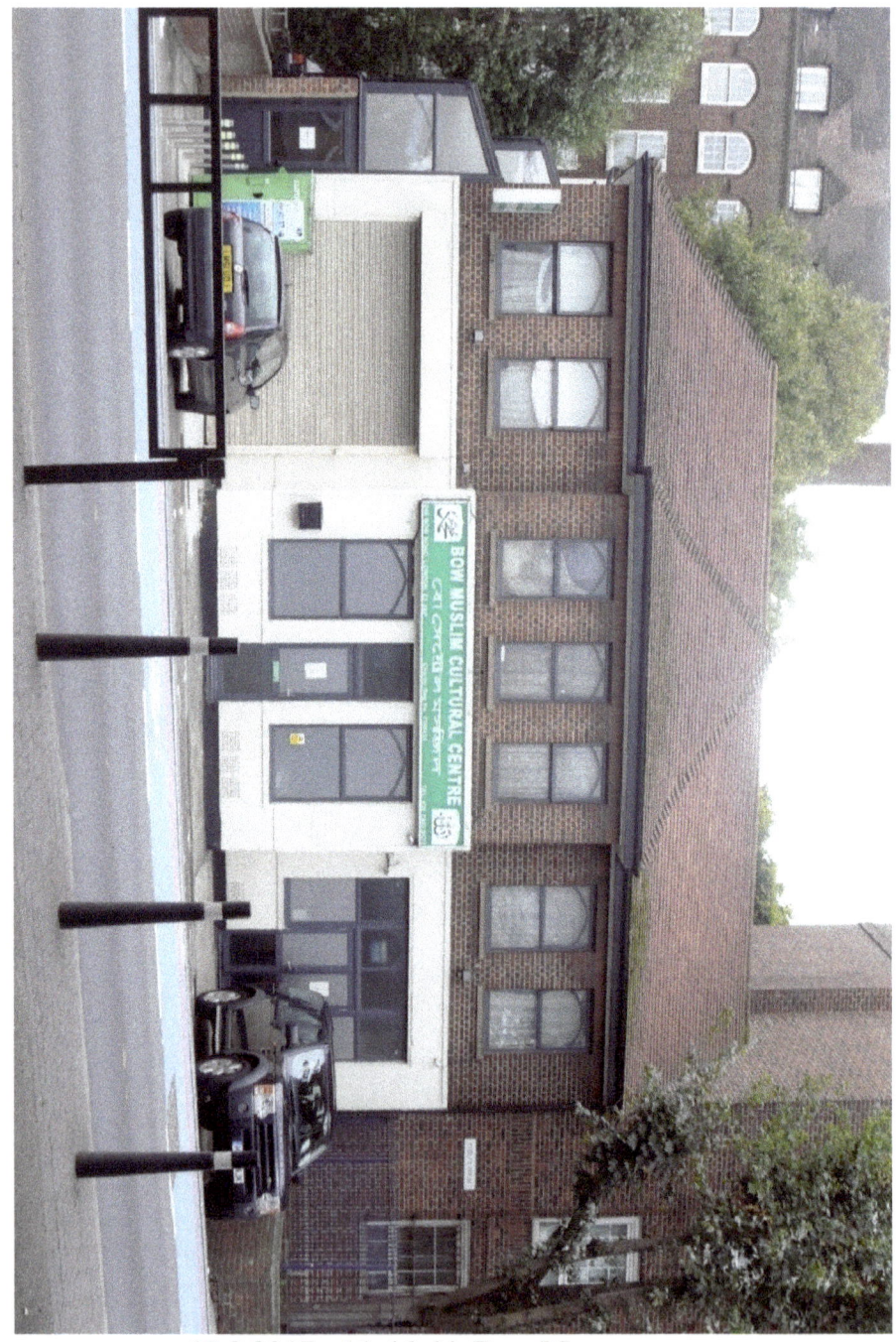

17.9.2017 - 11:46:44, Bow Mosque

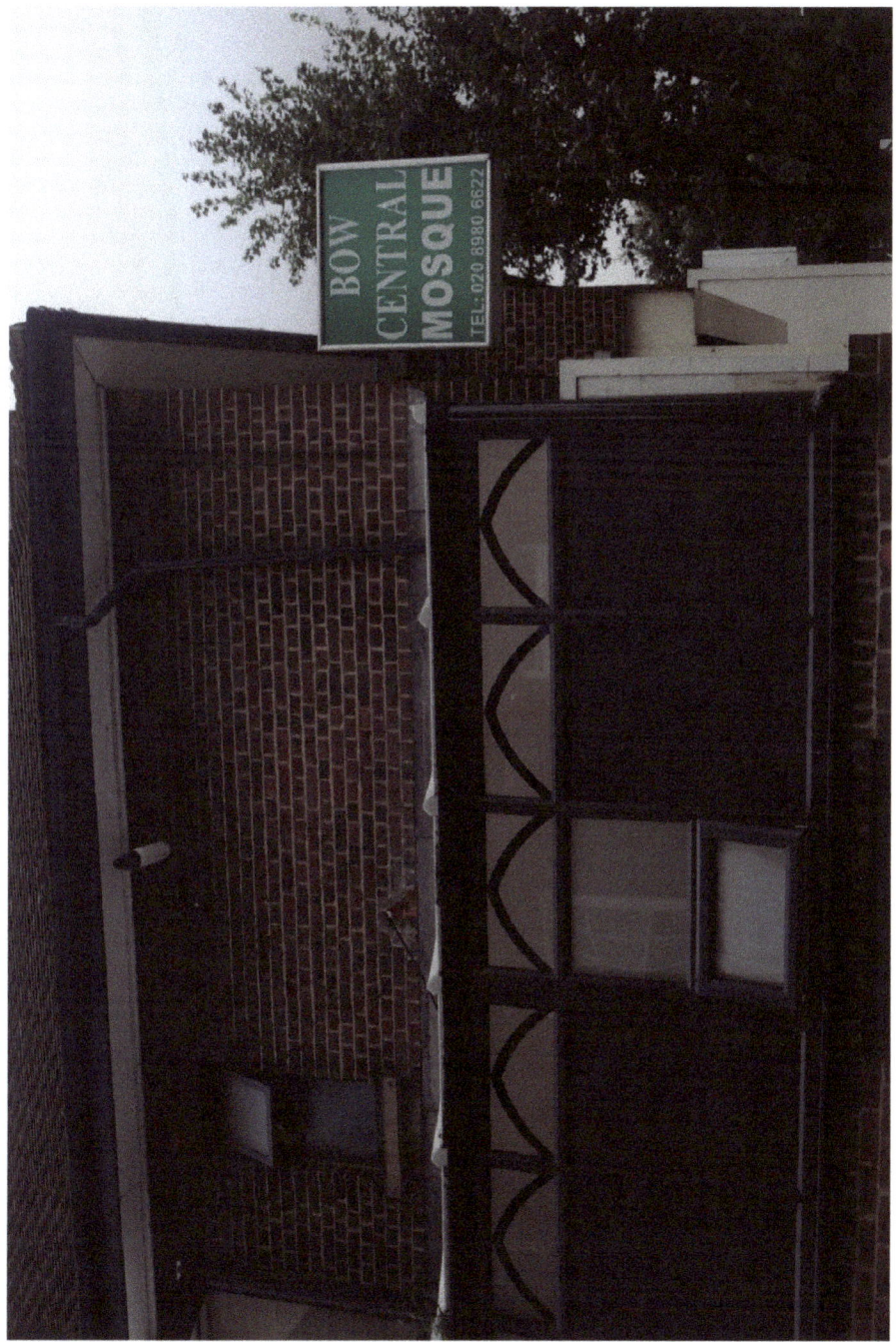

17.9.2017 - 11:47:32, Bow Mosque side view

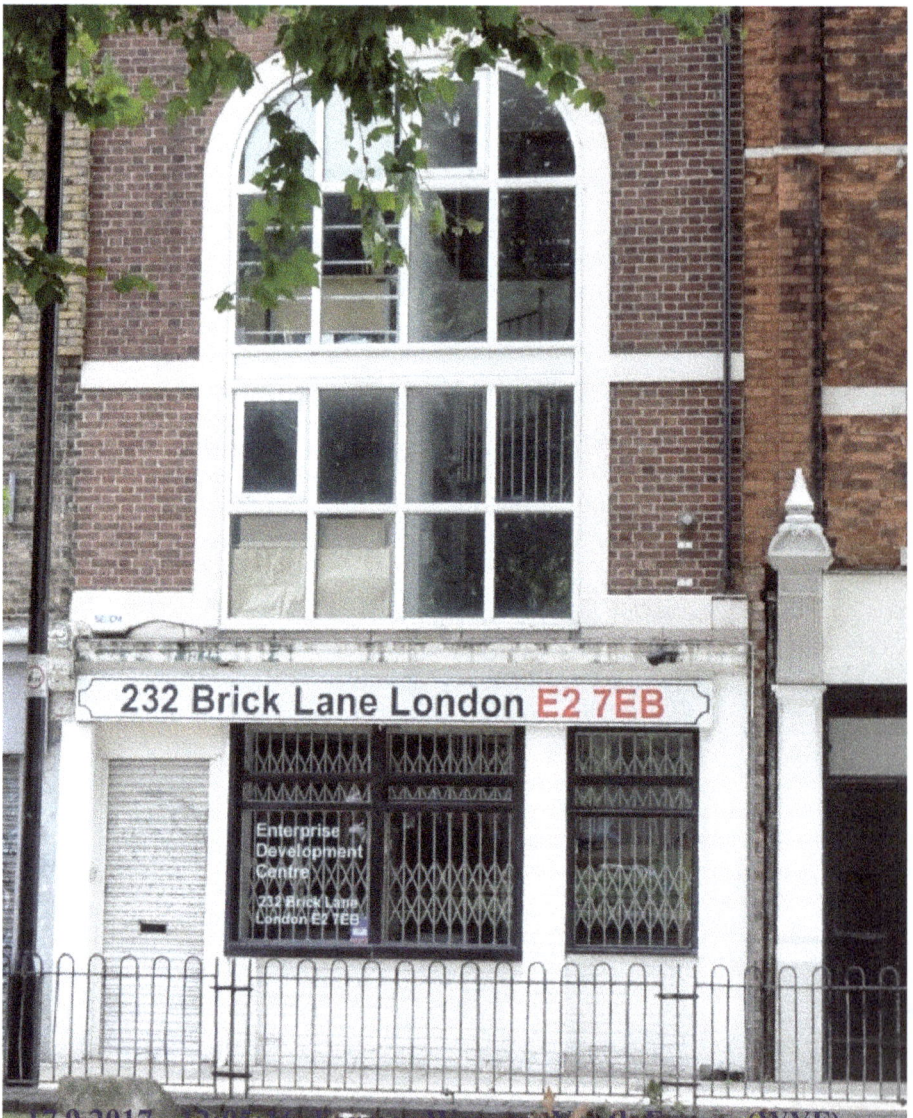

17.9.2017 - 12:05:16, Former Weavers Youth Forum (WYF) building

This is the organisation that supported my growing up till my late teens, through the holiday programmes and other community initiatives. I'm indebted to my local youth and voluntary organisations, WYF, Boundary Community School and St Hilda's east.

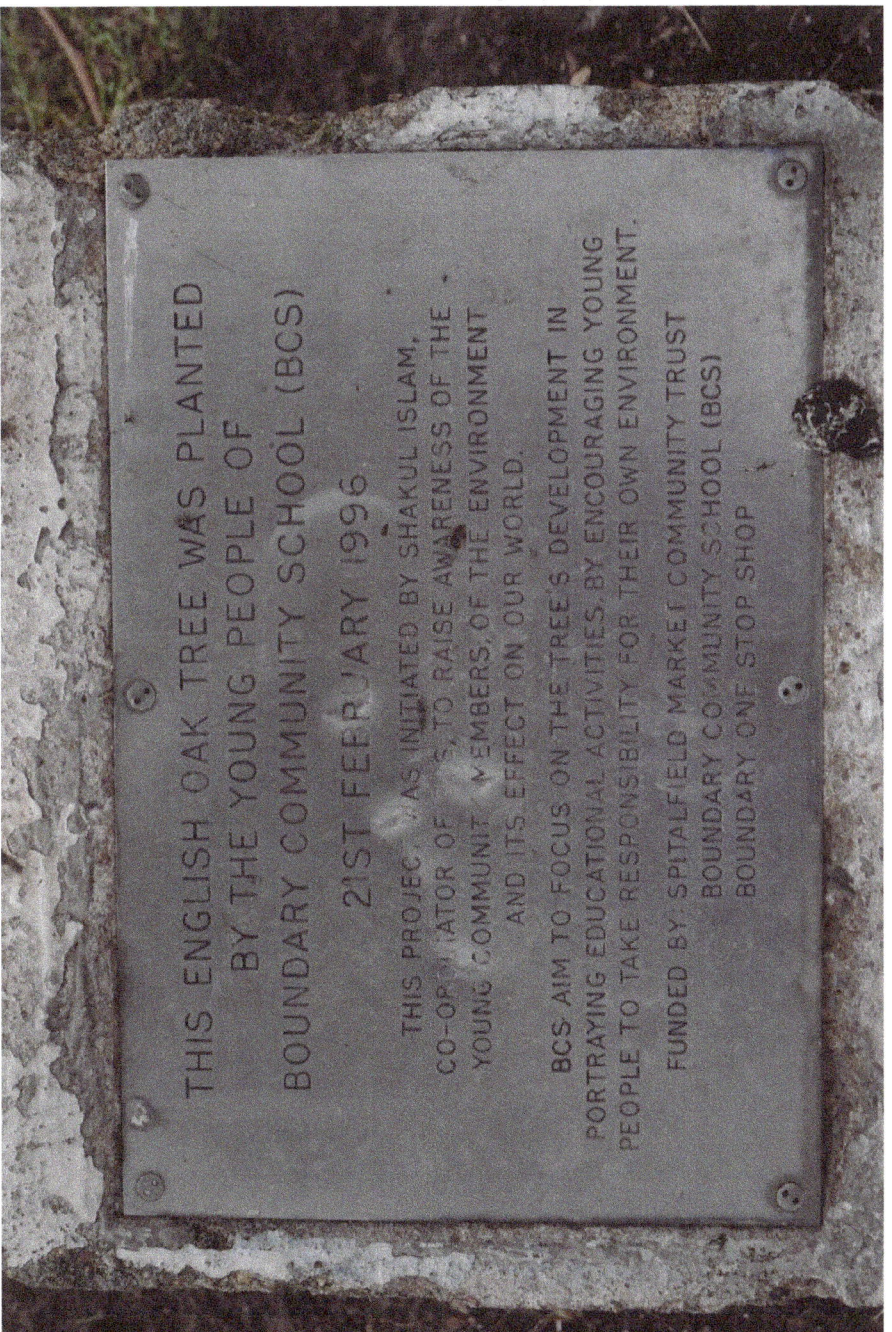

17.9.2017 - 12:05:54, Plaque Opposite the WFY Building

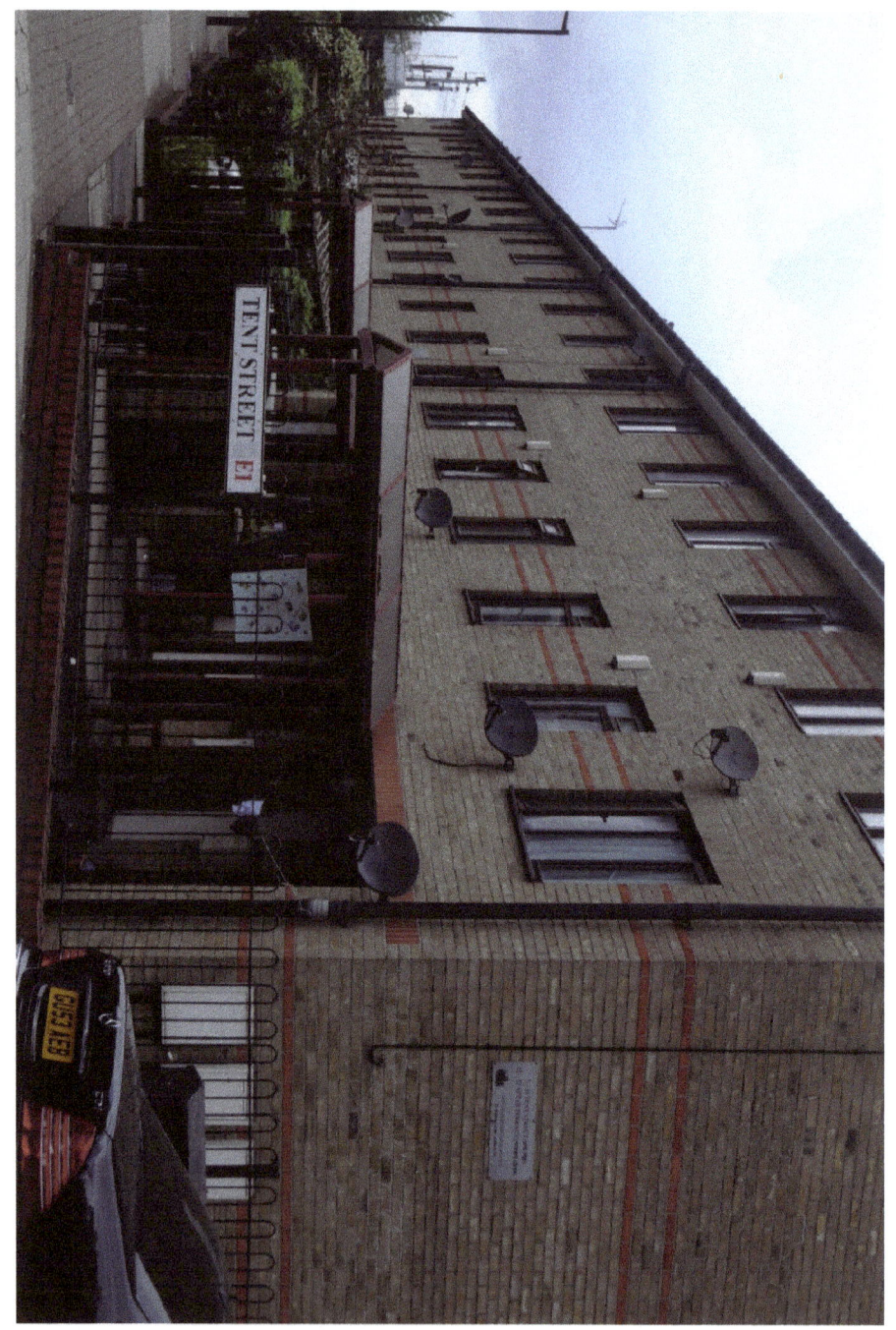

17.9.2017 - 12:16:10, Aftab Terrace on Tent Street.

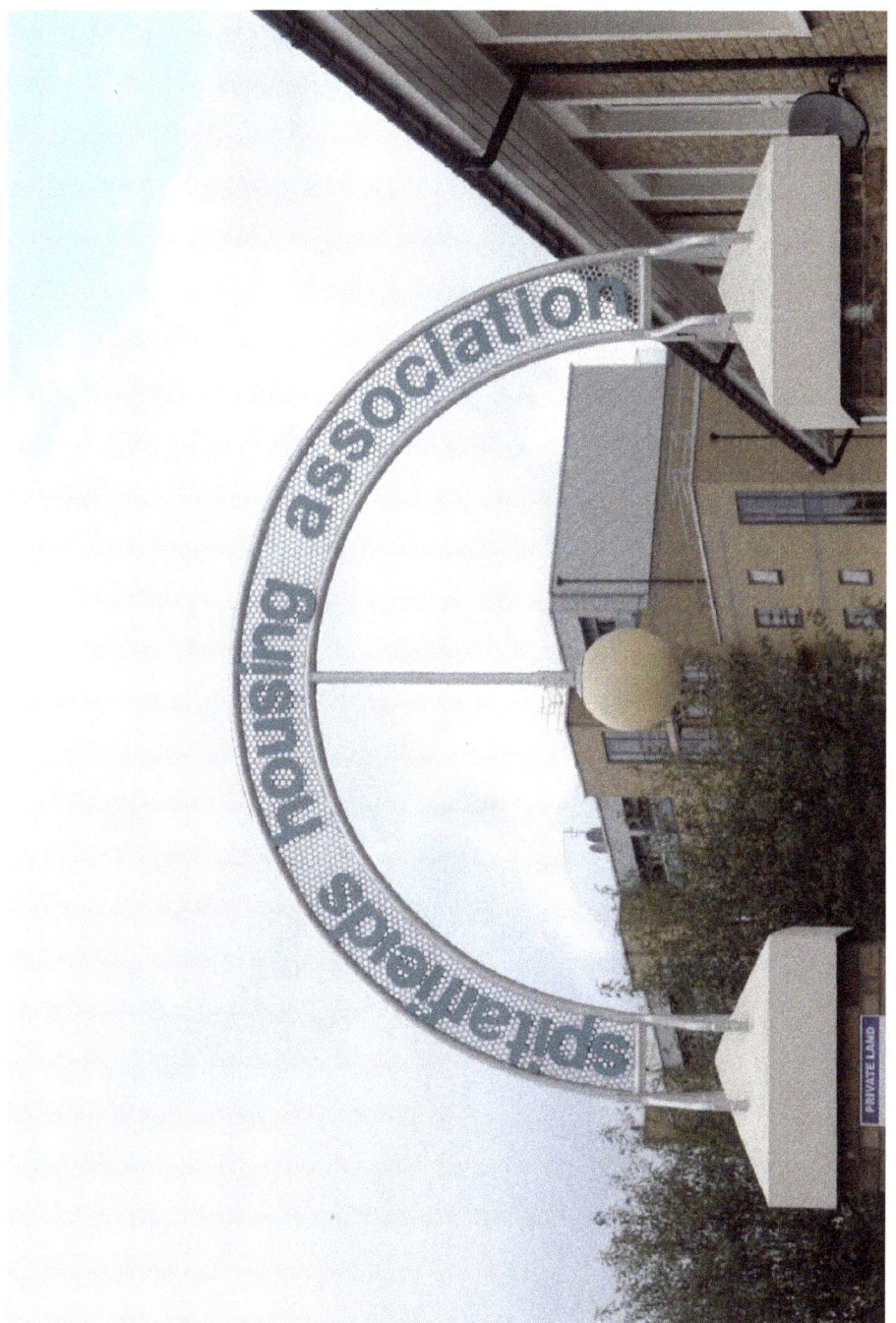

17.9.2017 - 12:18:14,

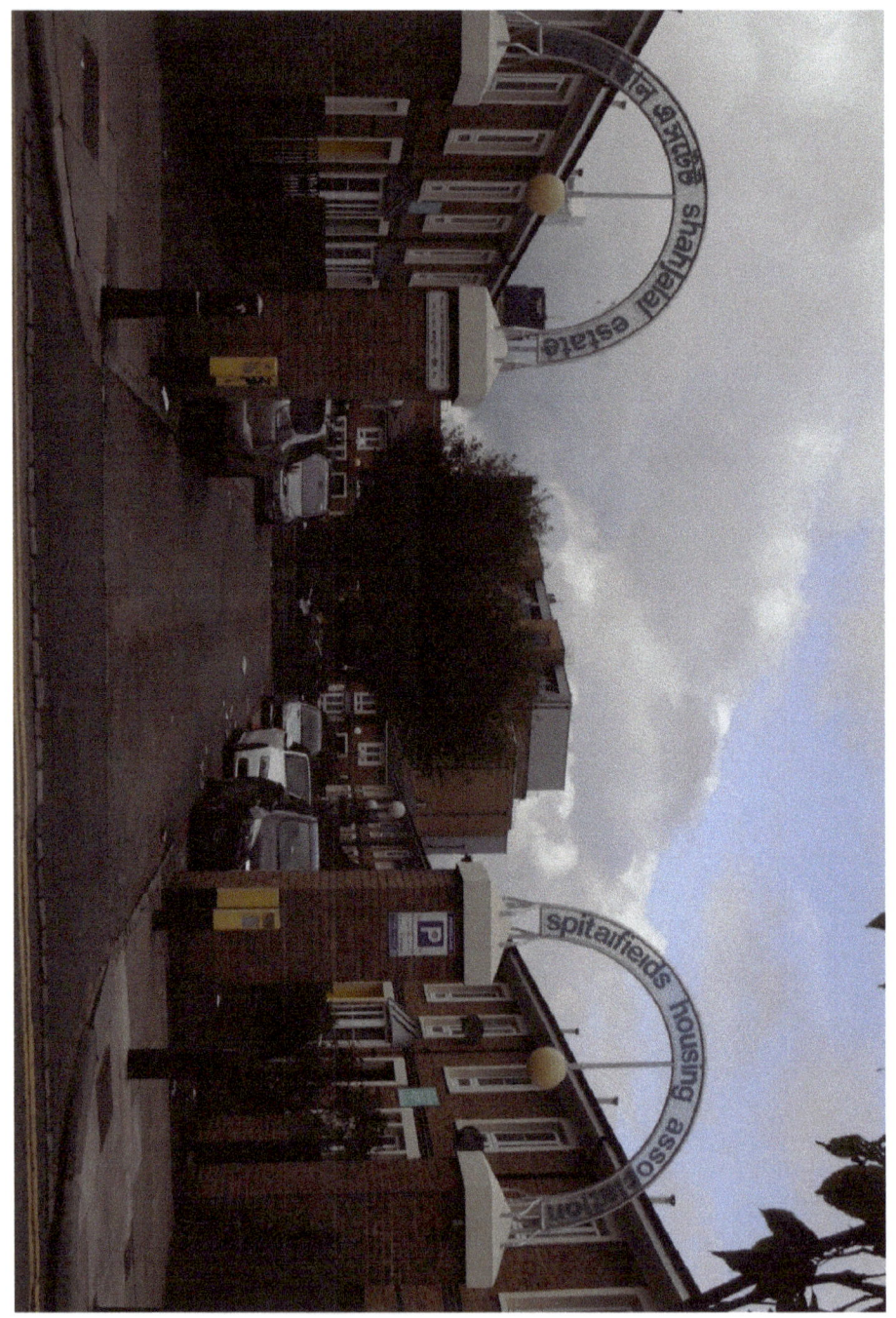

17.9.2017 - 12:18:46

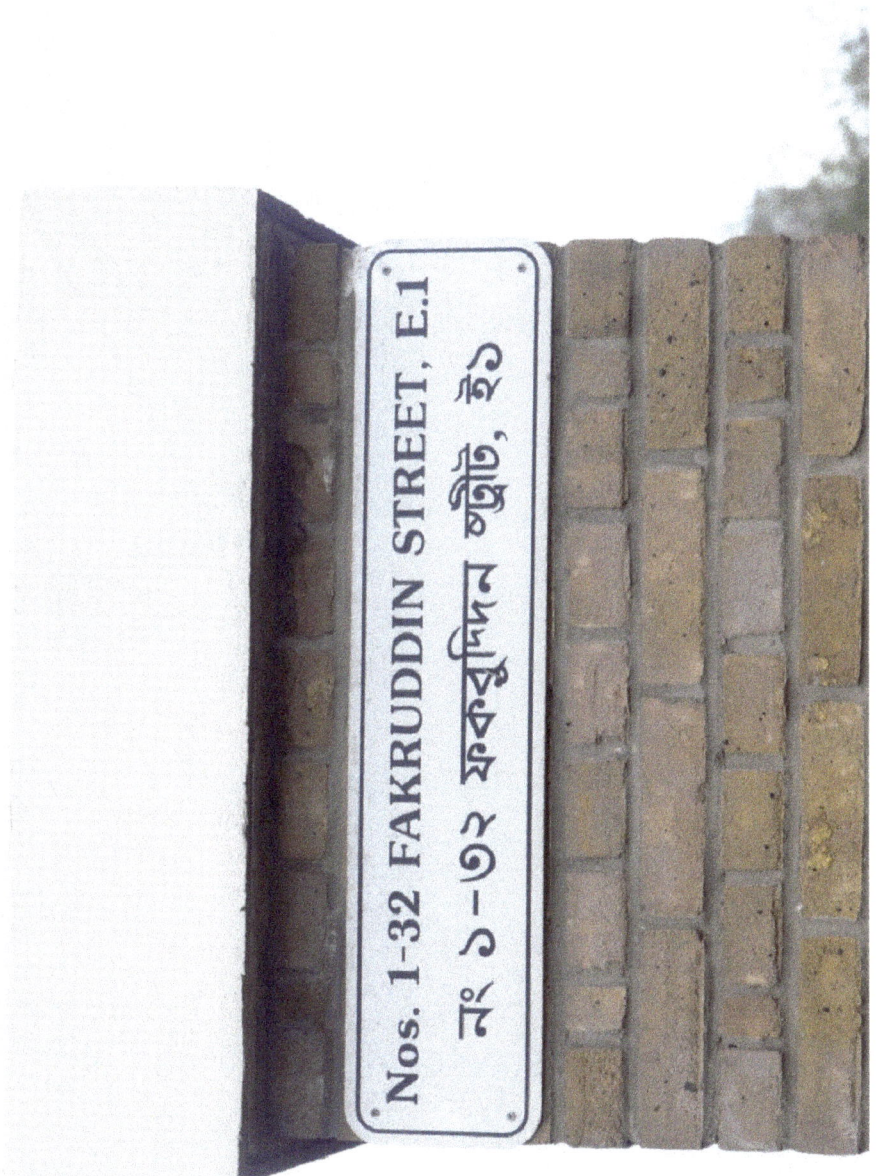

17.9.2017 - 12:19:14

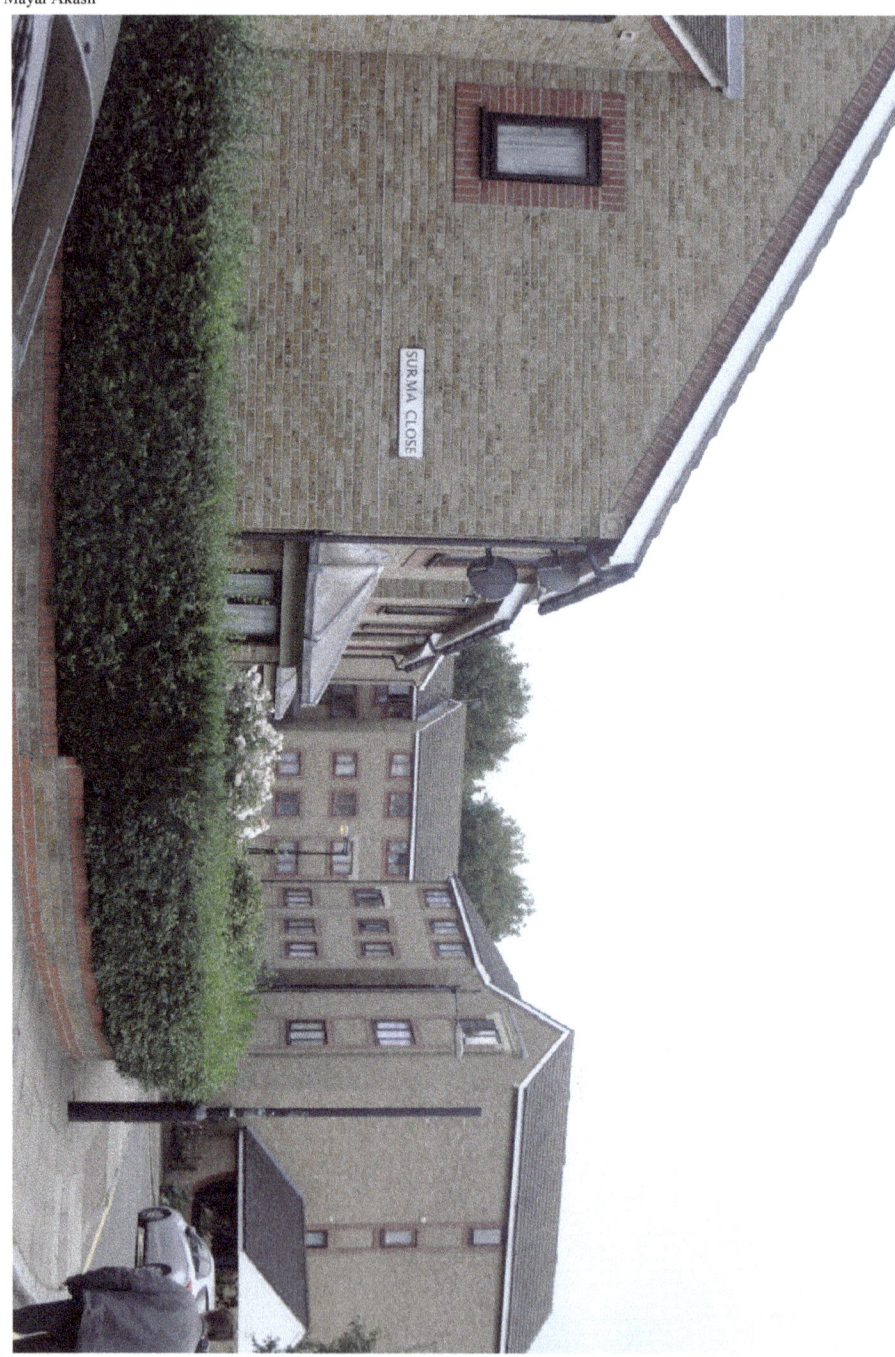

17.9.2017 - 12:21:22, Surma Close

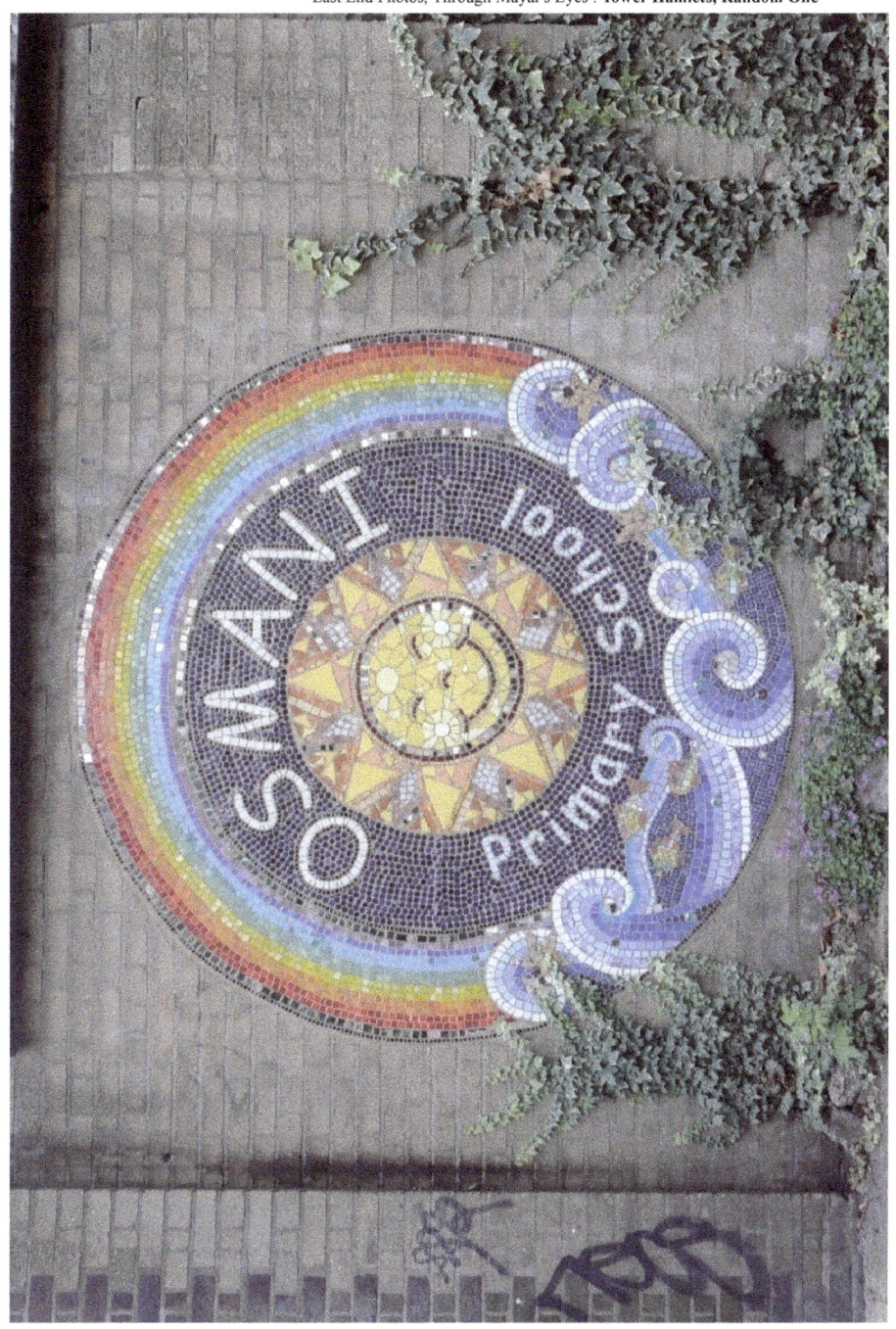

17.9.2017 - 12:27:28

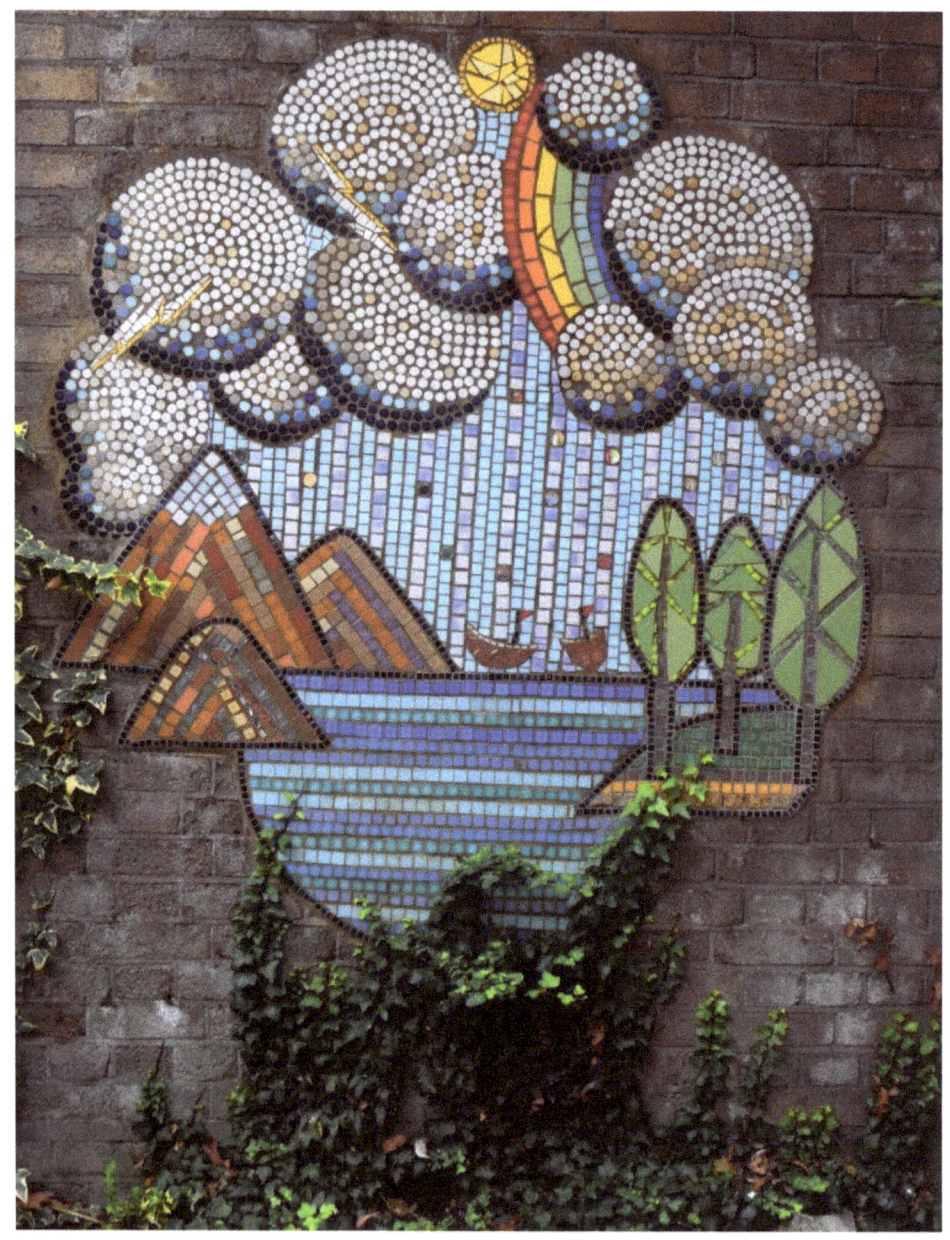

17.9.2017 - 12:28

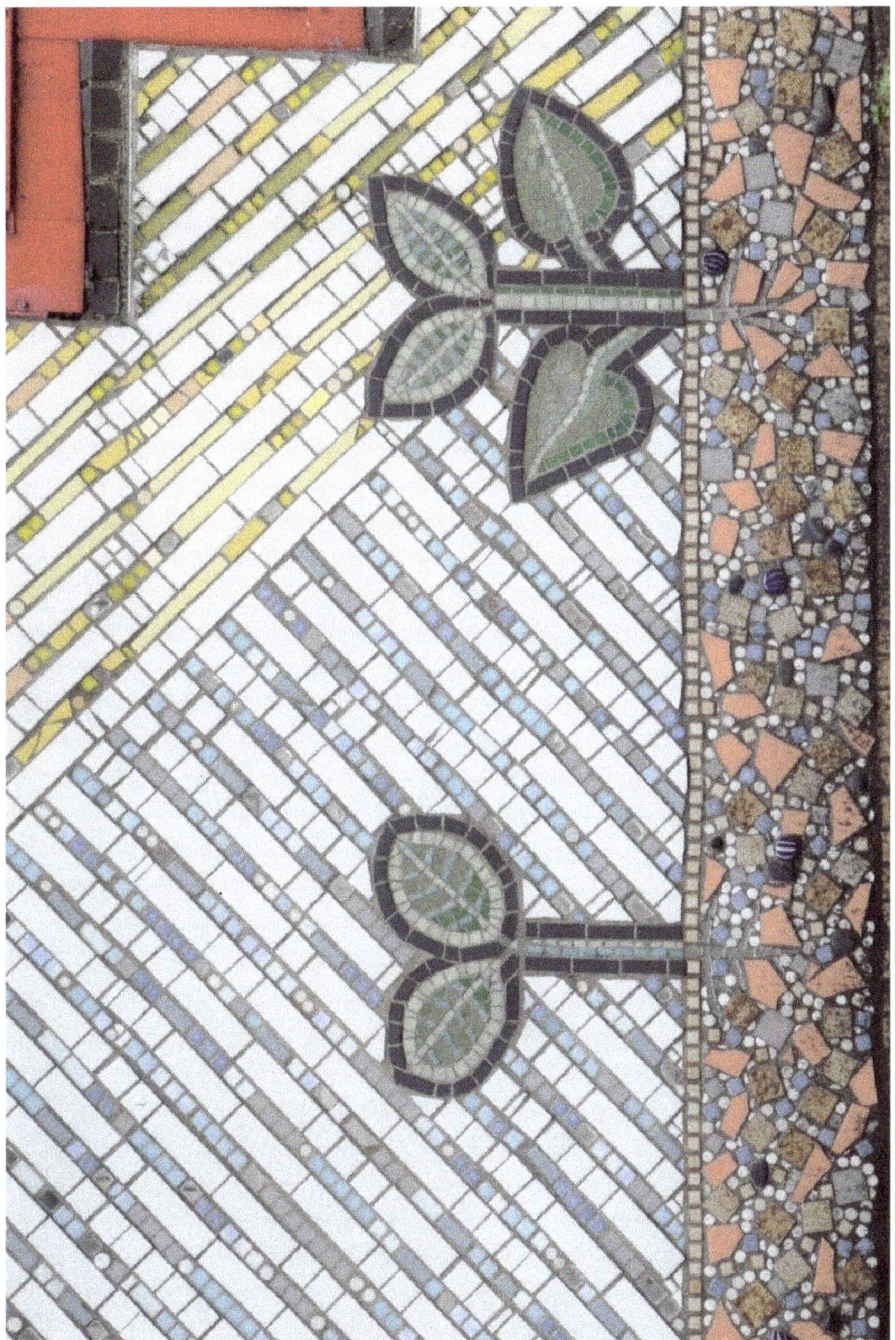

17.9.2017 - 12:28:26, **Mural of Osmani School**

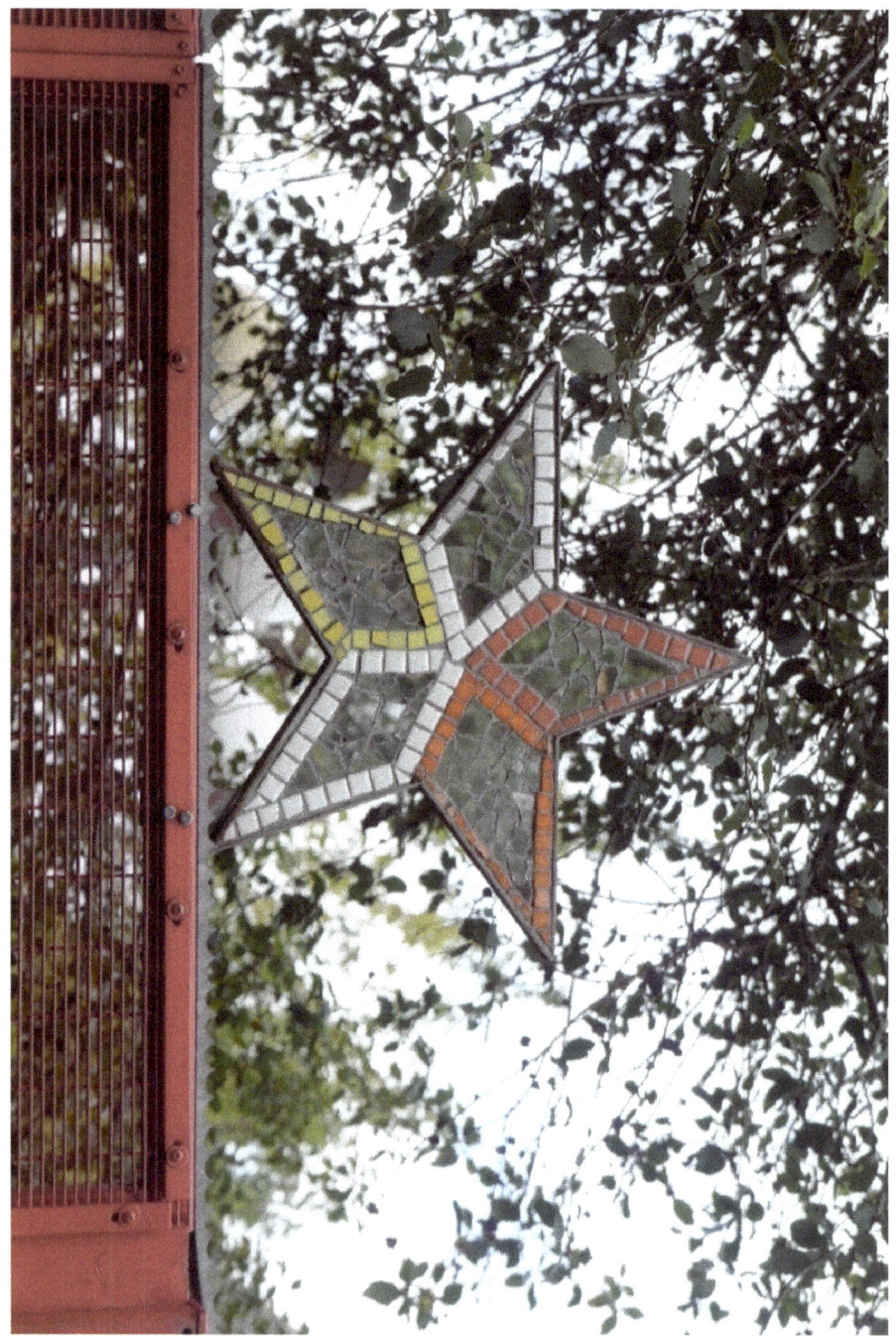

17.9.2017 - 12:28:36, Osmani School Star

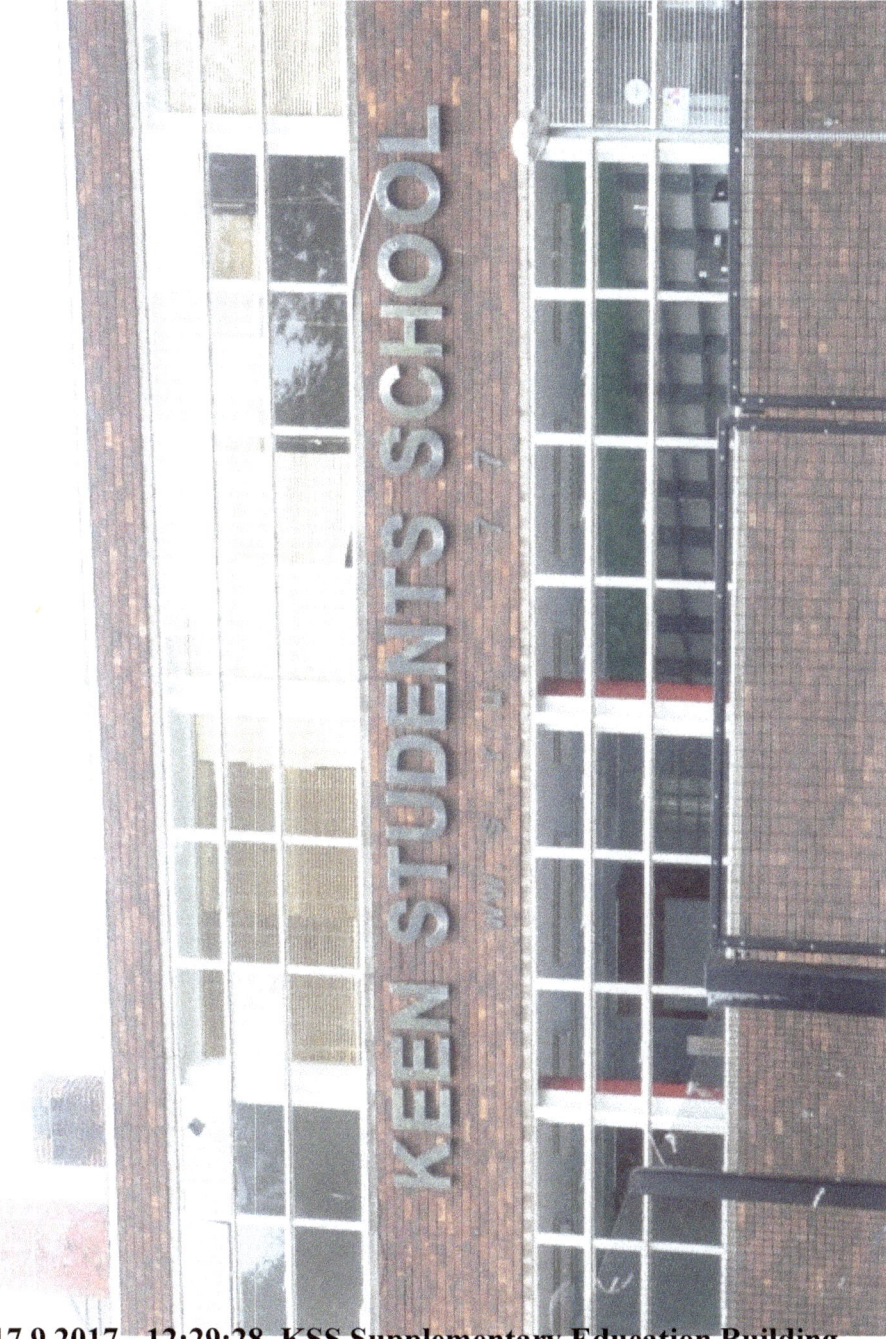

17.9.2017 - 12:29:28, KSS Supplementary Education Building, Valance Road.

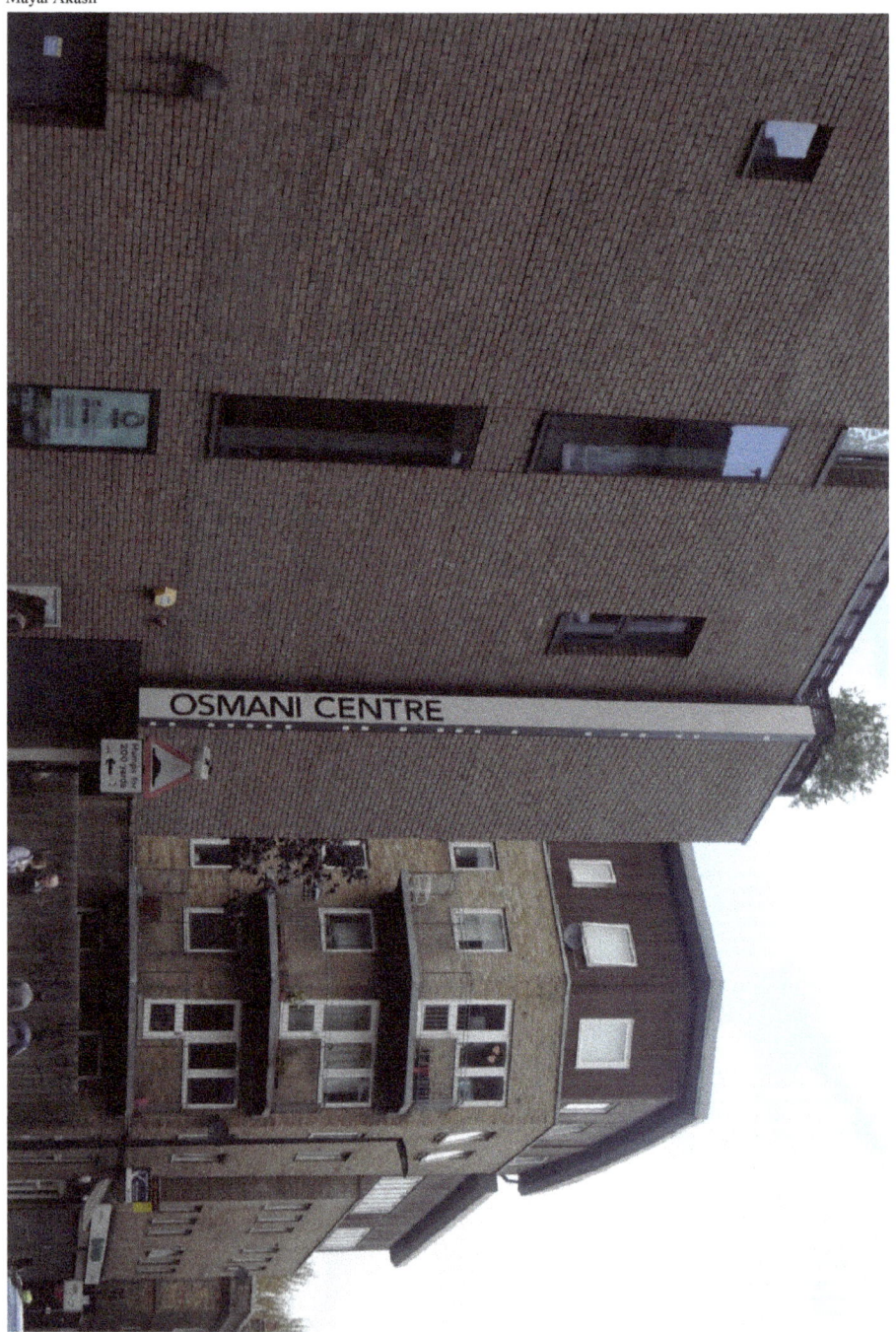

17.9.2017 - 12:29:50, Valance Road, Osmani Centre

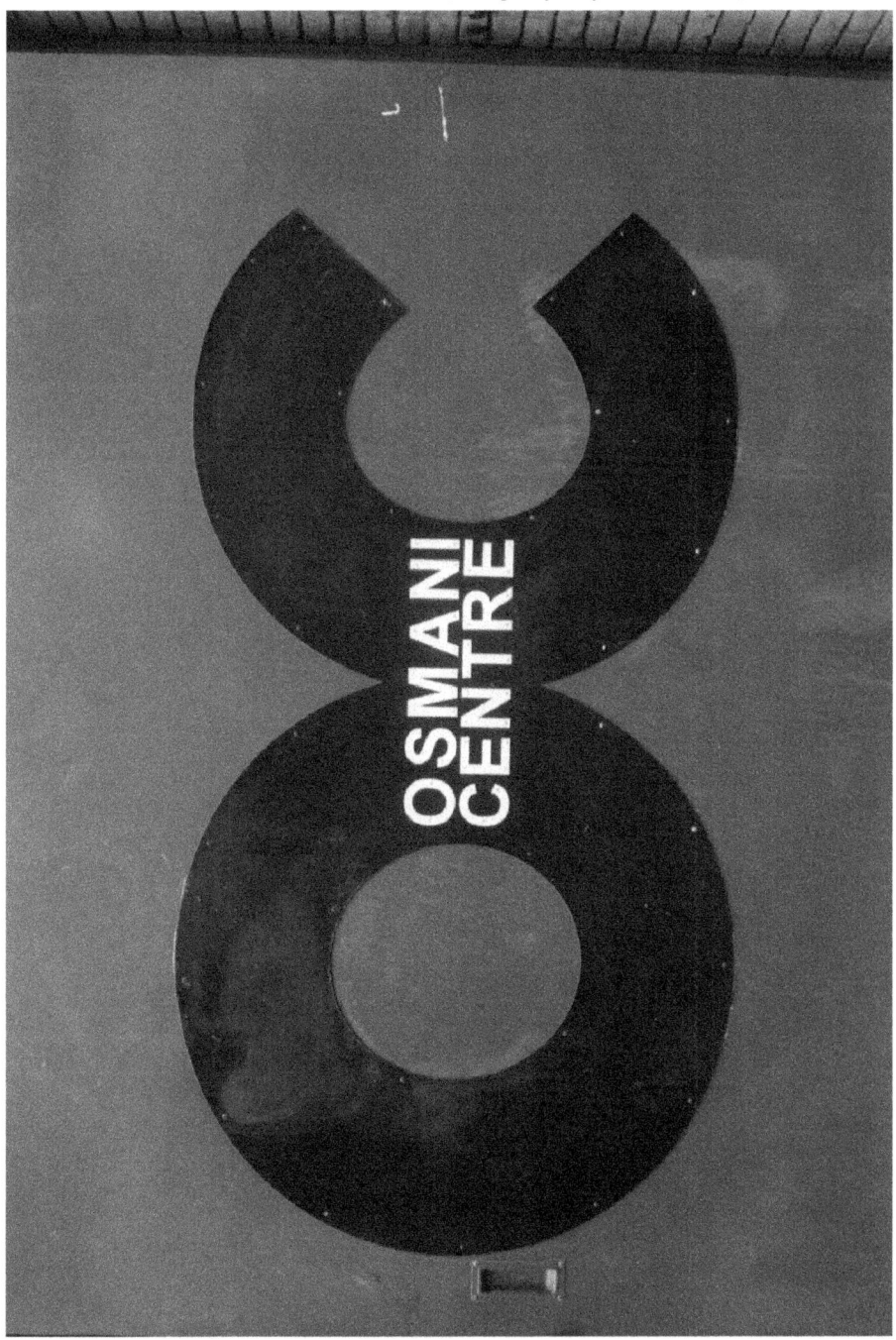

17.9.2017 - 12:24:46

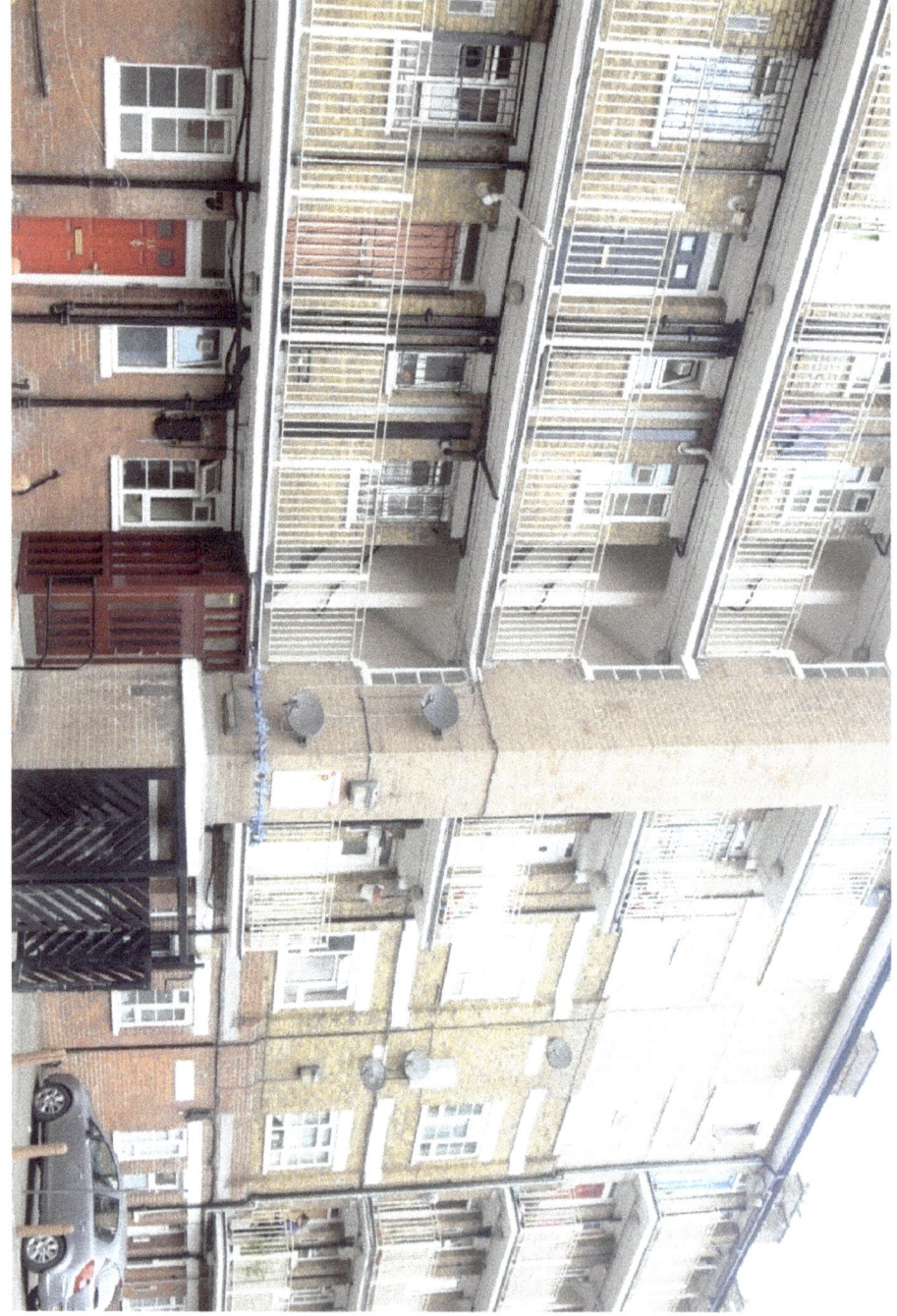

17.9.2017 - 12:30:22, Valance Road, Hughes Mansion

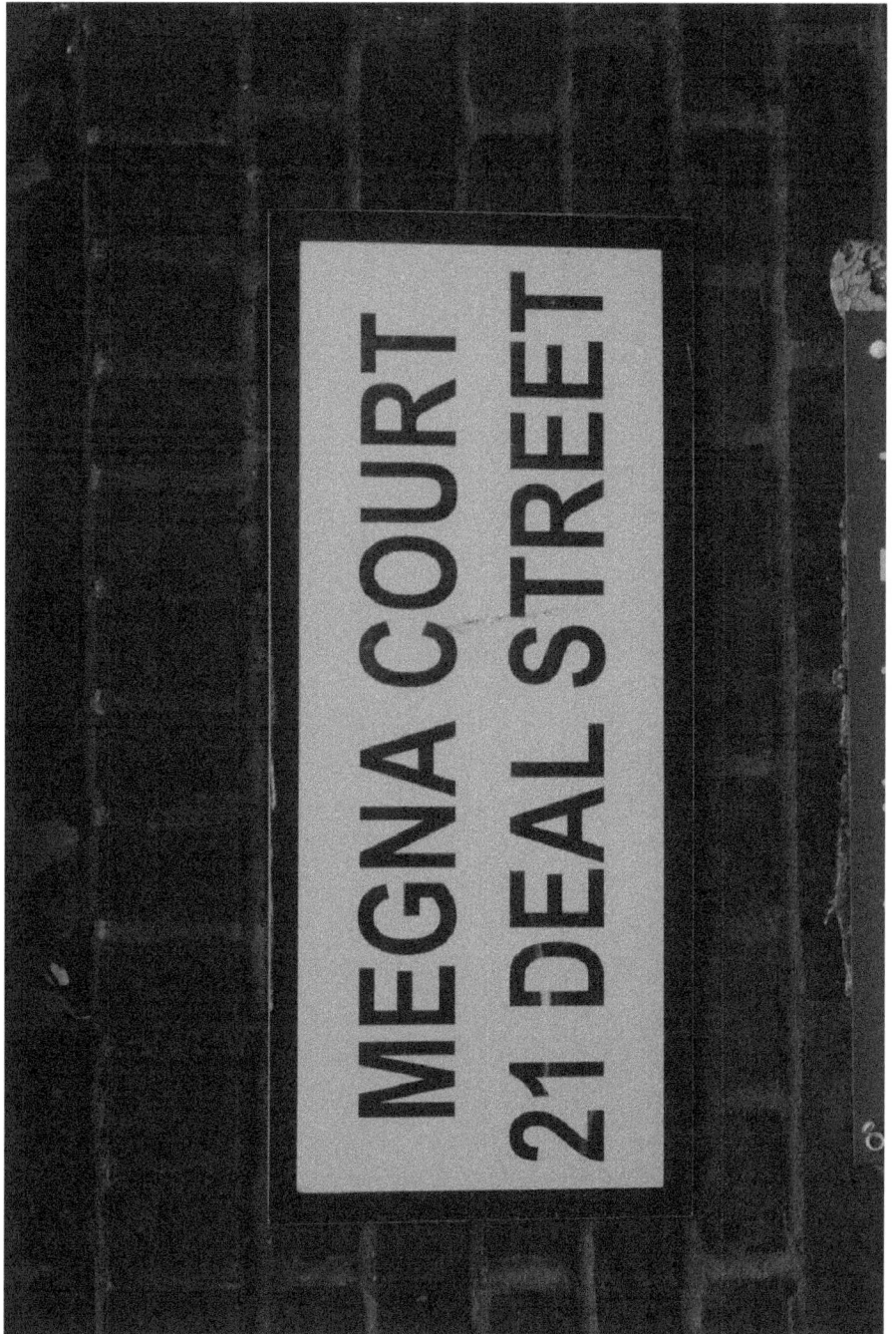

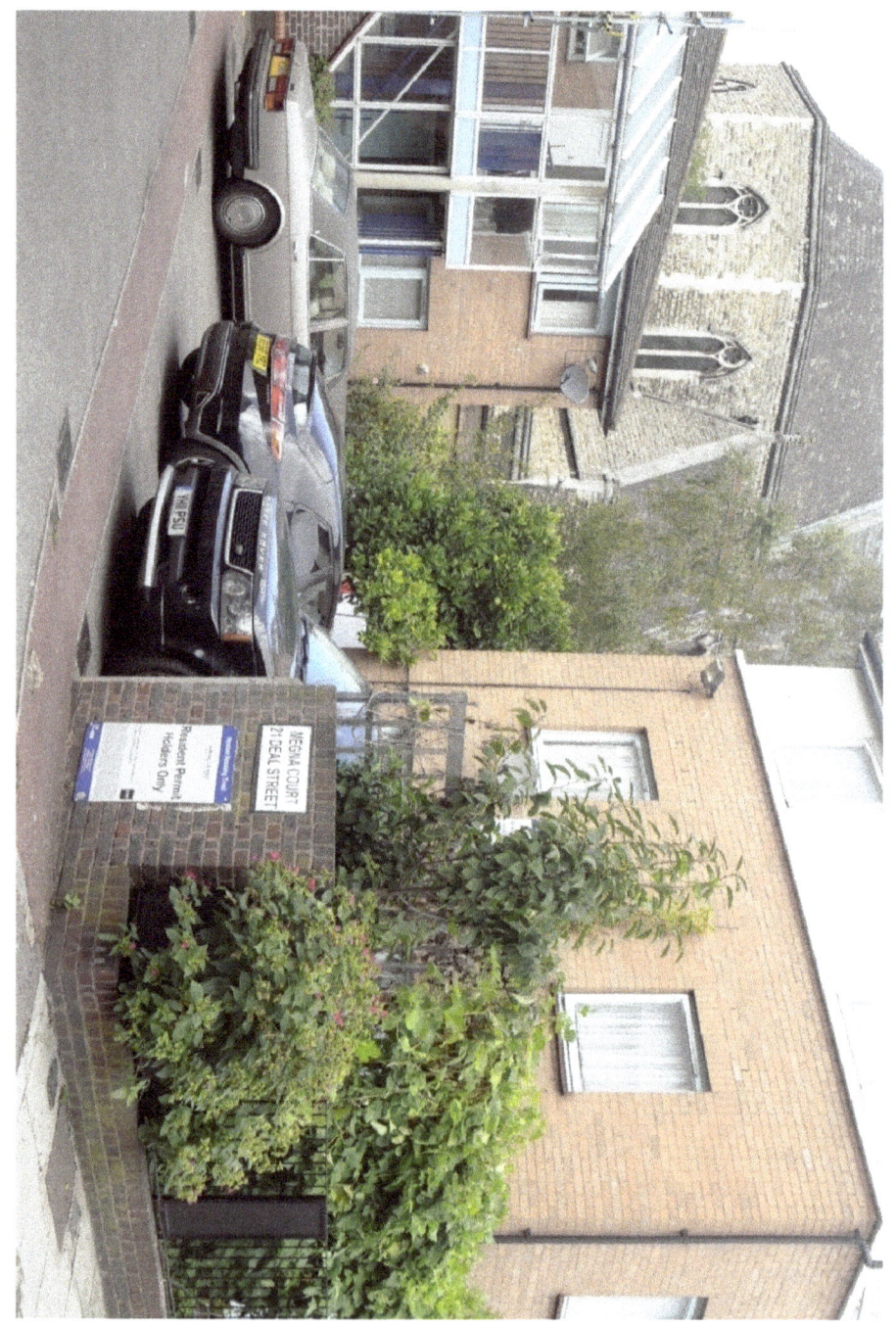

17.9.2017 - 12:33:30 Megna Close, Deal Street

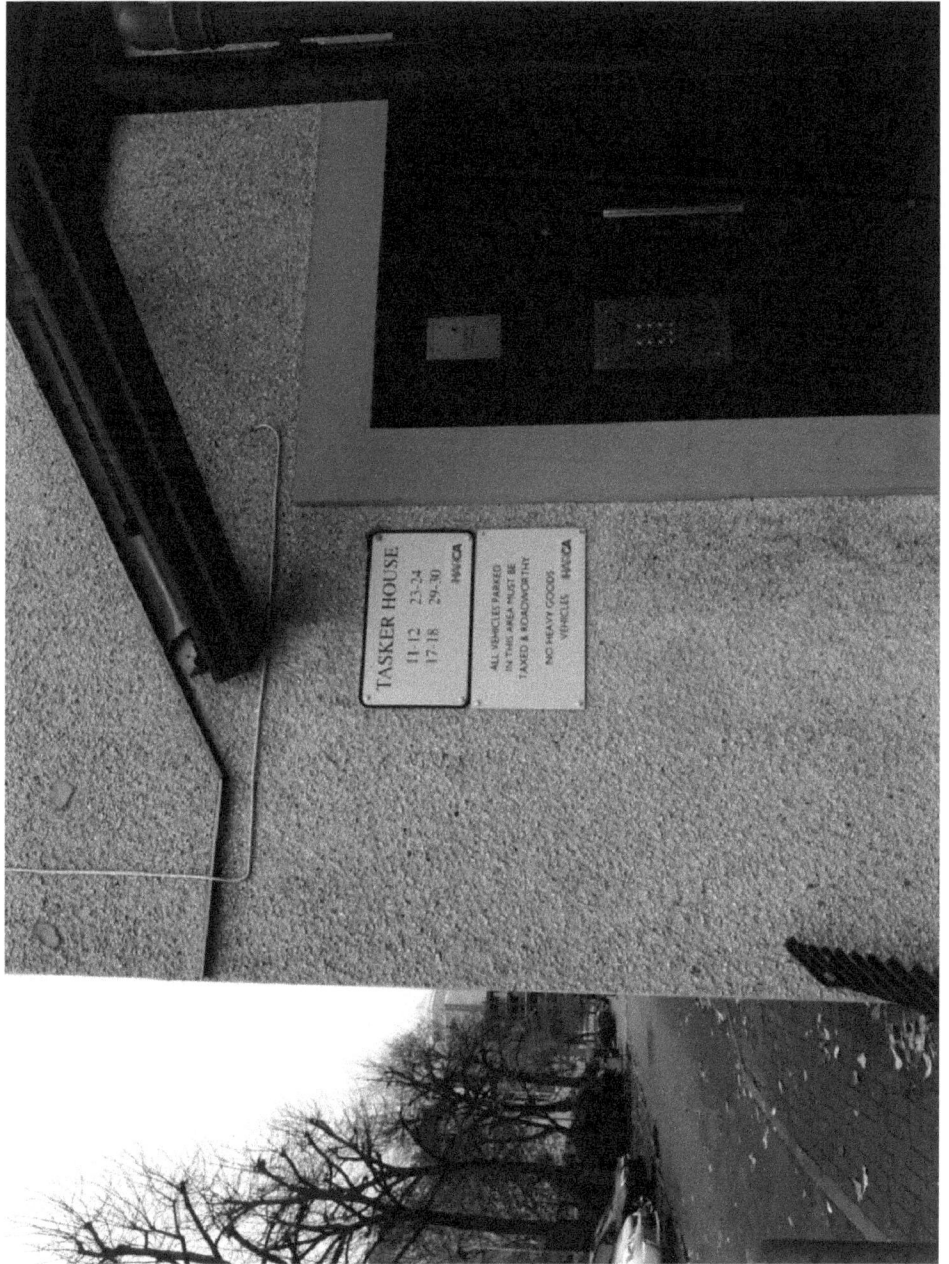

20.11.2017 - 13:13:19, Burdett Estate

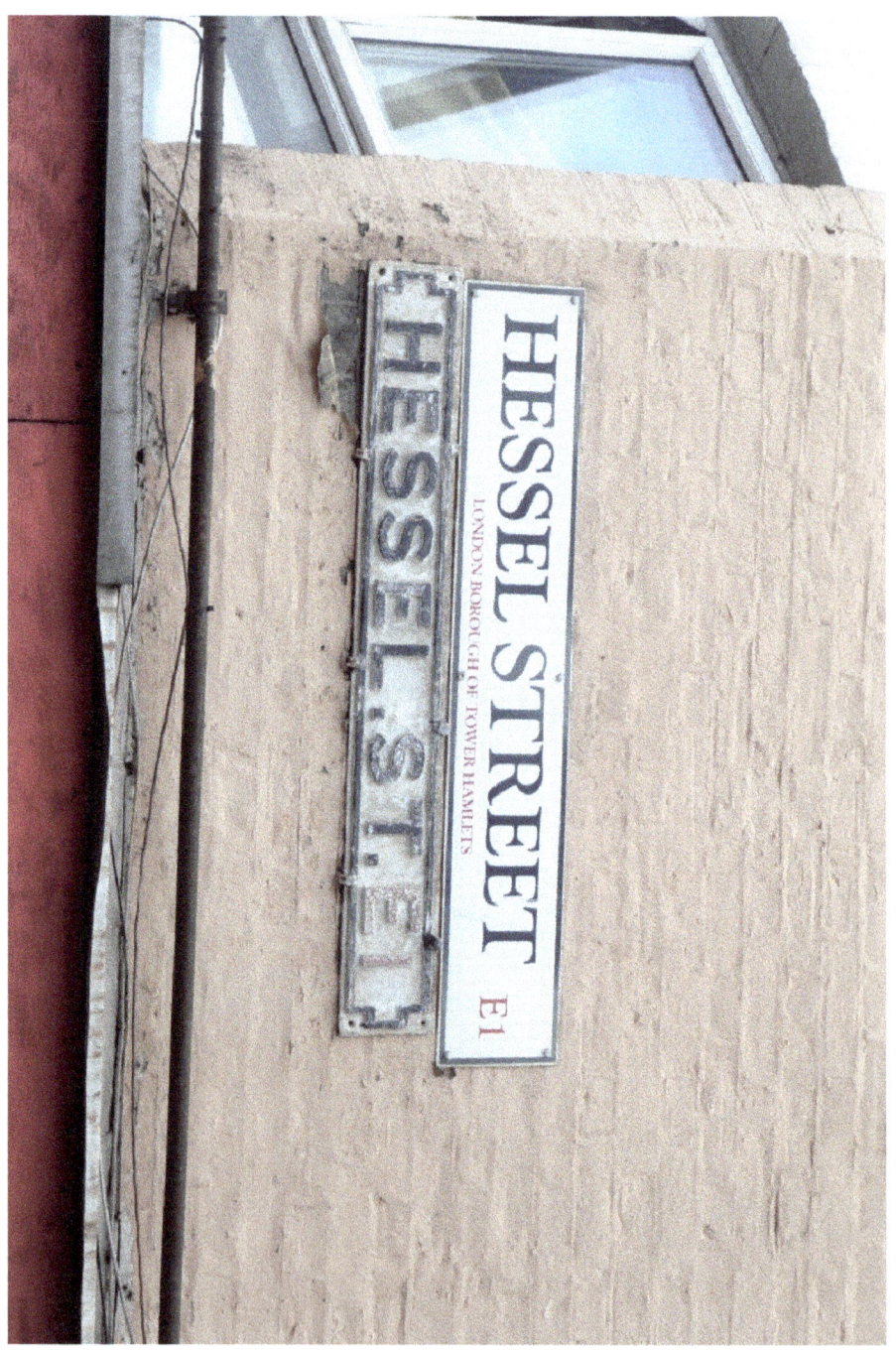

17.9.2017 - 13:26:10

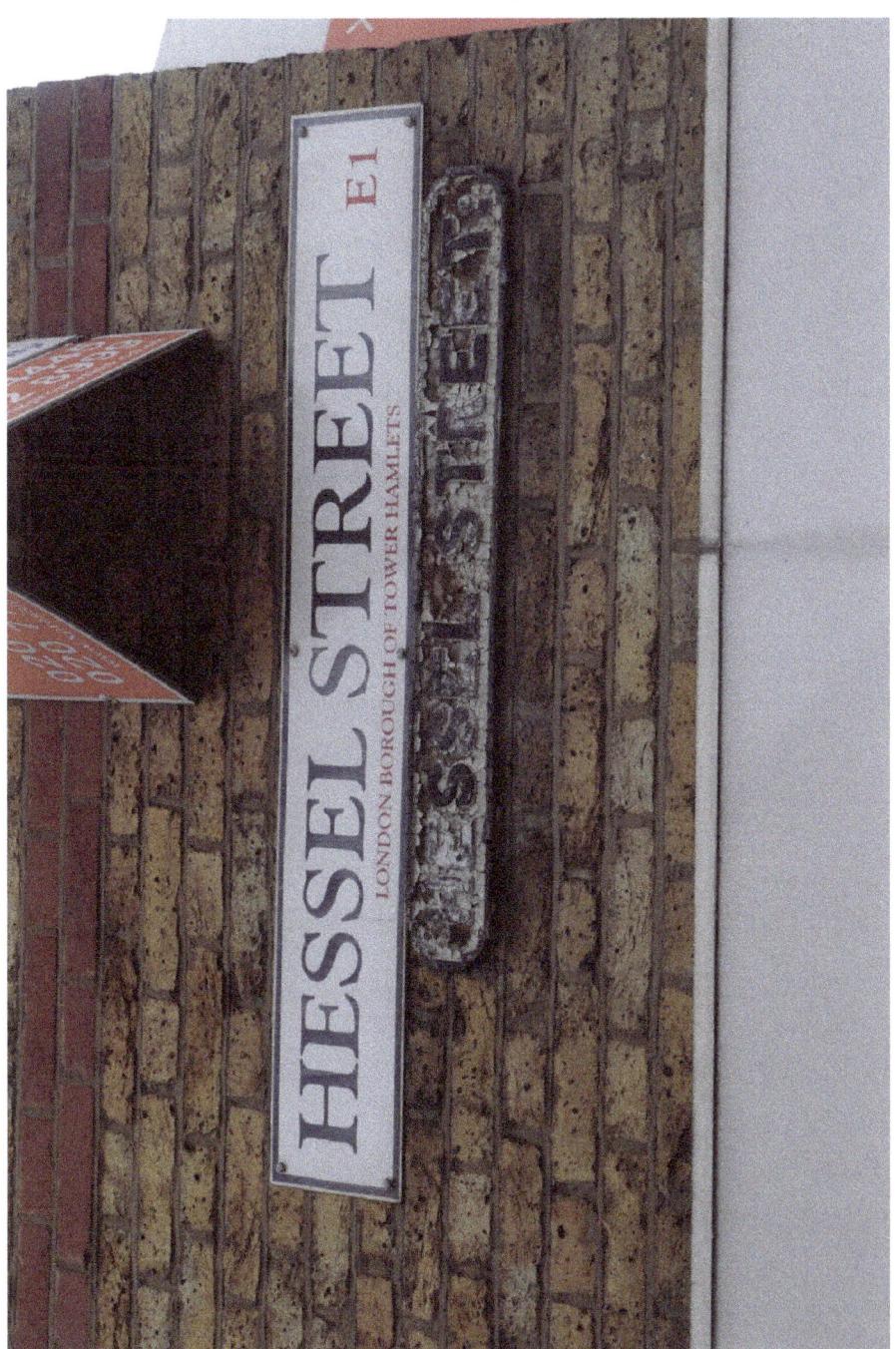

17.9.2017 - 13:26:32

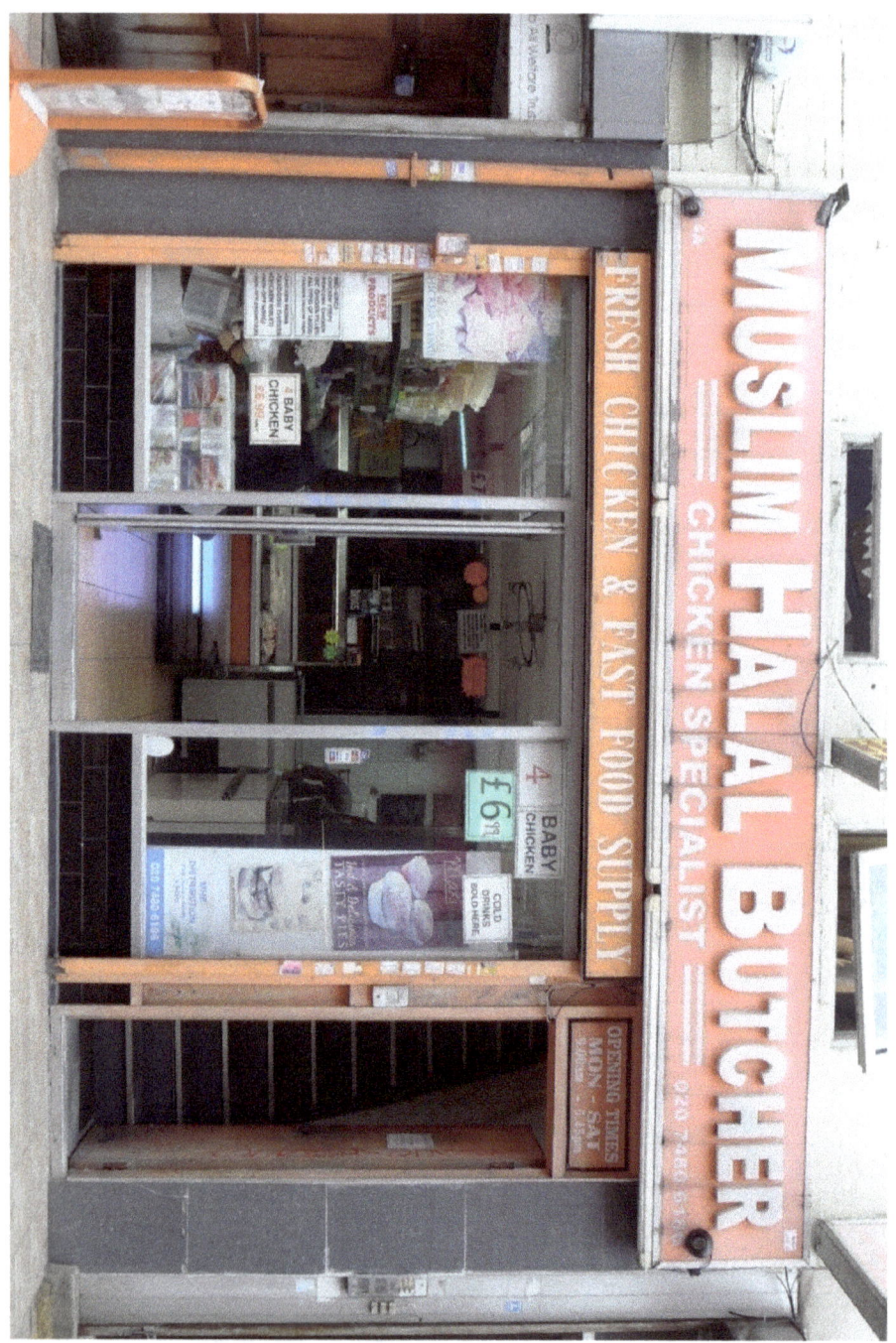

17.9.2017 - 13:26:58, Hessel Street

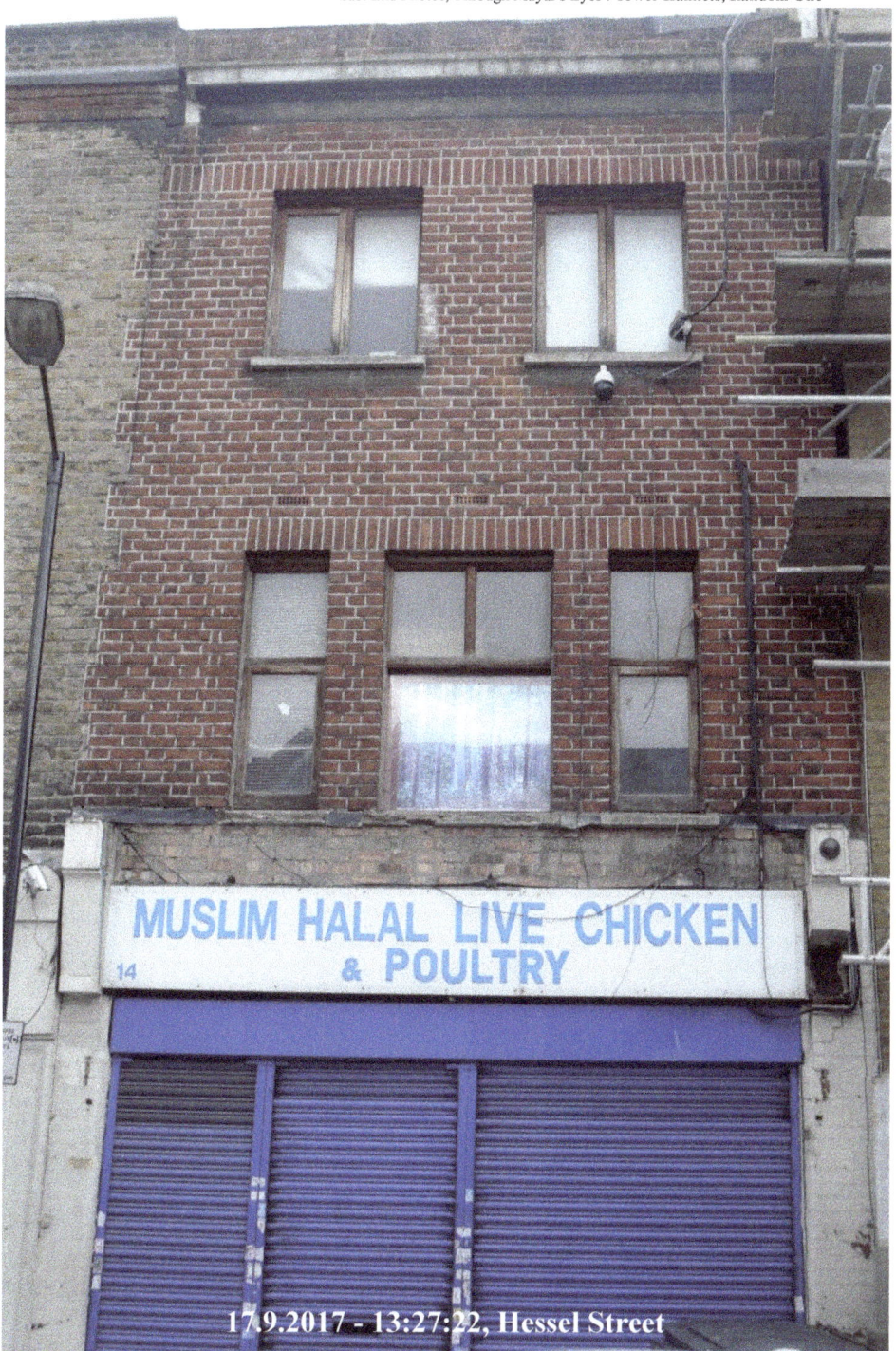

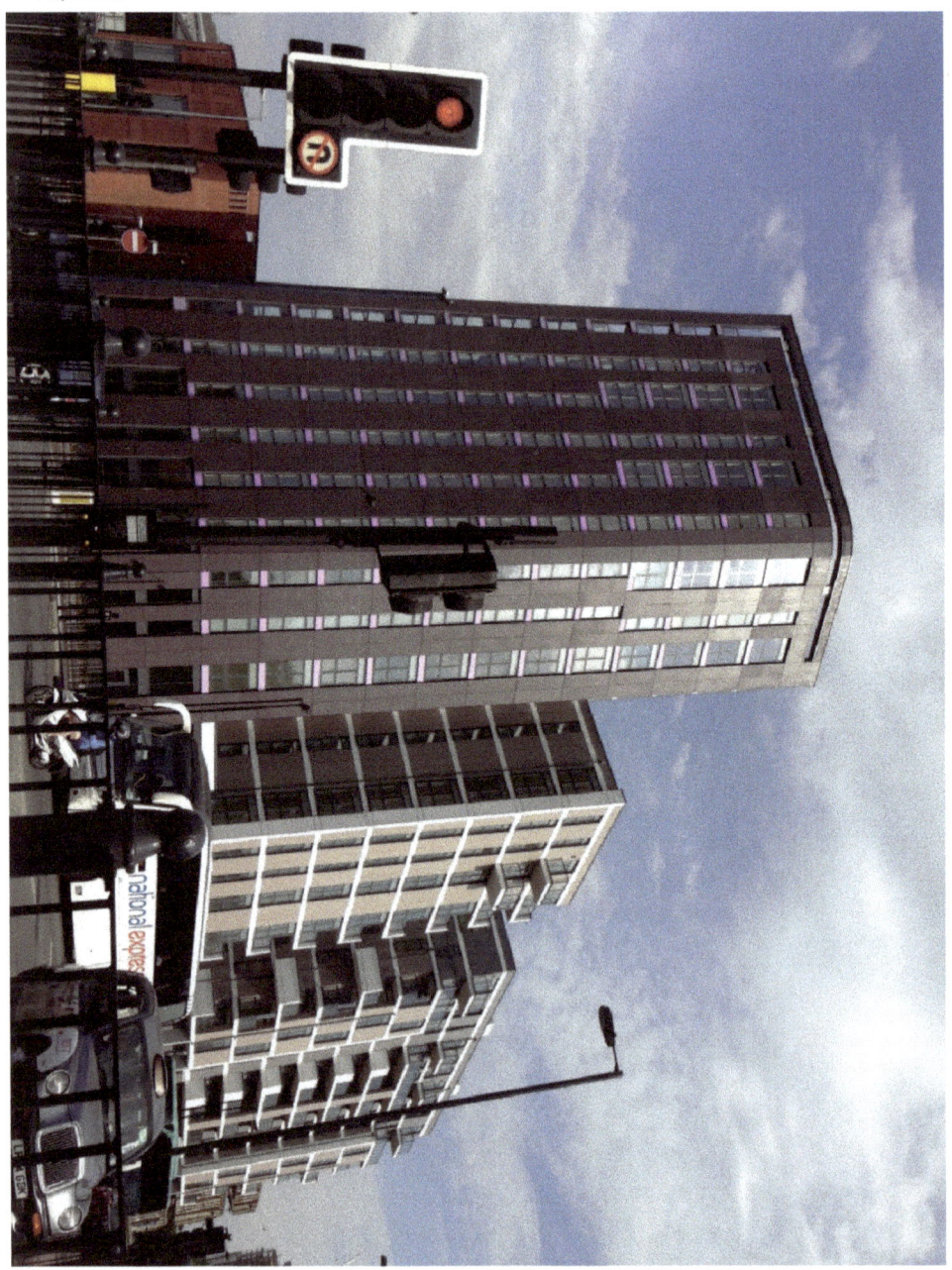

1.7.2015 - 17:09, East India Dock Road

East End Photos, Through Mayar's Eyes : **Tower Hamlets, Random One**

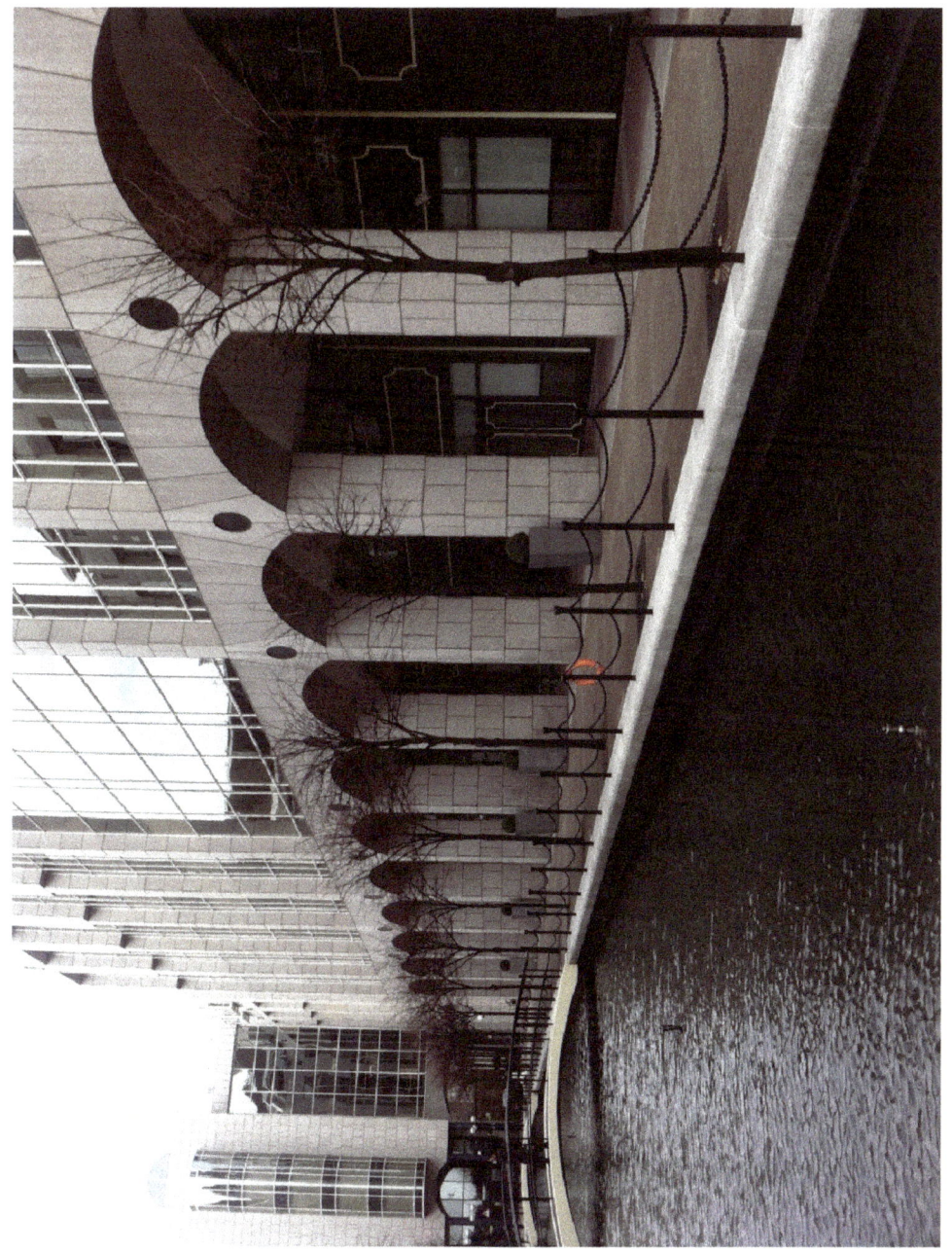

13.4.2013 - 10:48, Mulberry Crescent

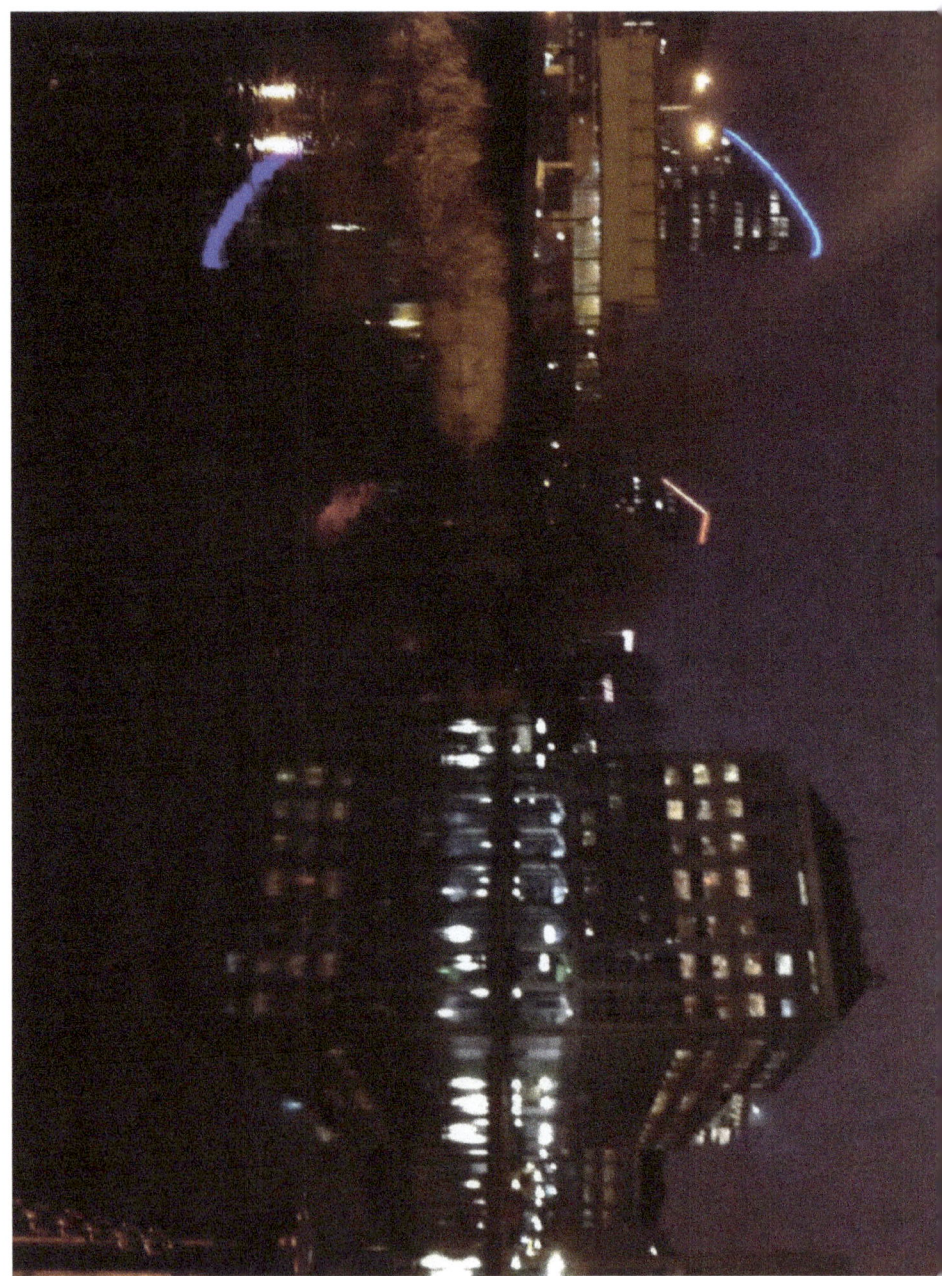

9.4.2013 - 20:25, Mulberry Crescent

East End Photos, Through Mayar's Eyes : **Tower Hamlets, Random One**

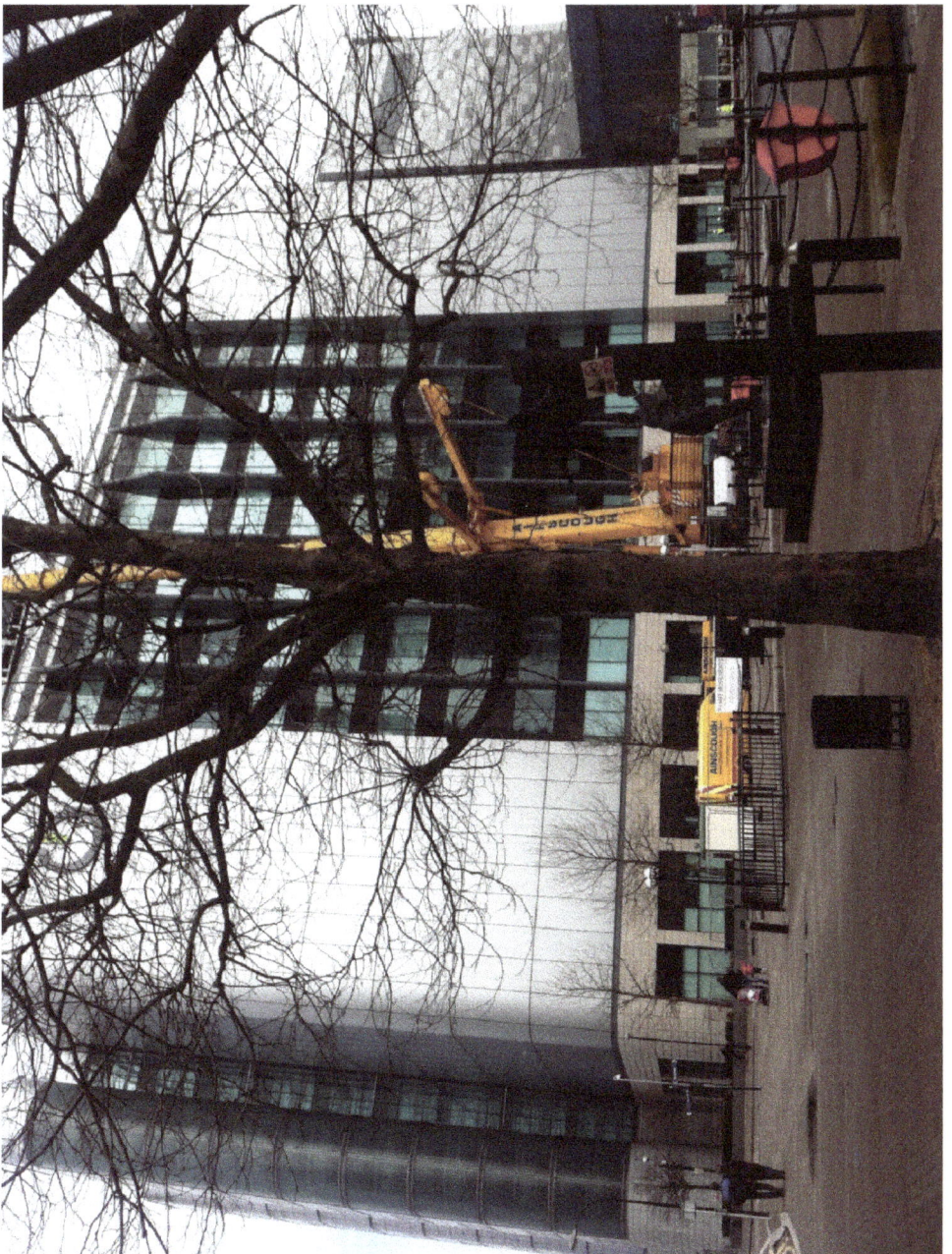

13.4.2013 - 10:47:53, Mulberry Crescent

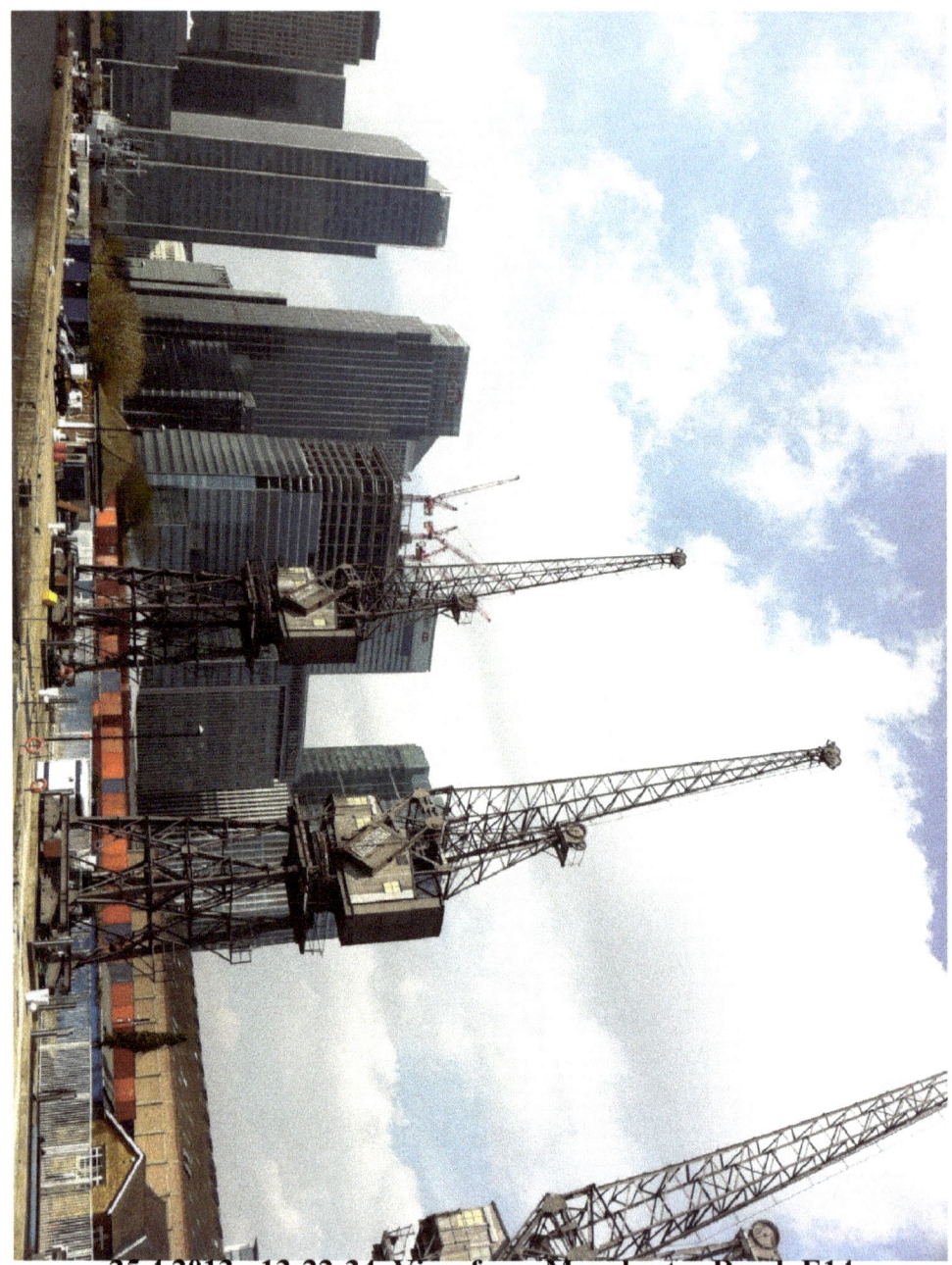

25.4.2013 - 13:22:34, View from Manchester Road, E14

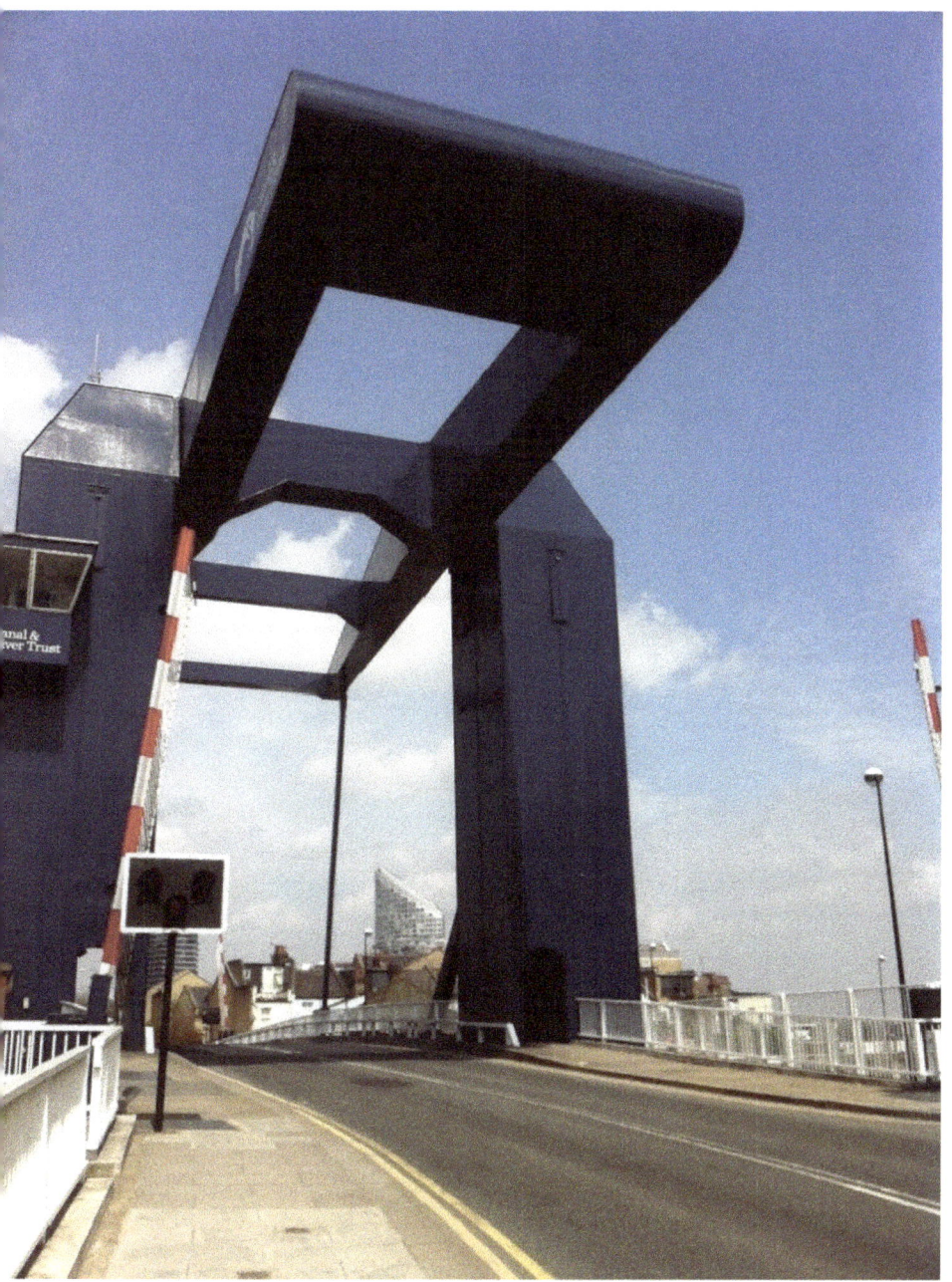

25.4.2013 - 13:21:22, Blue Bridge, Manchester Road, E14

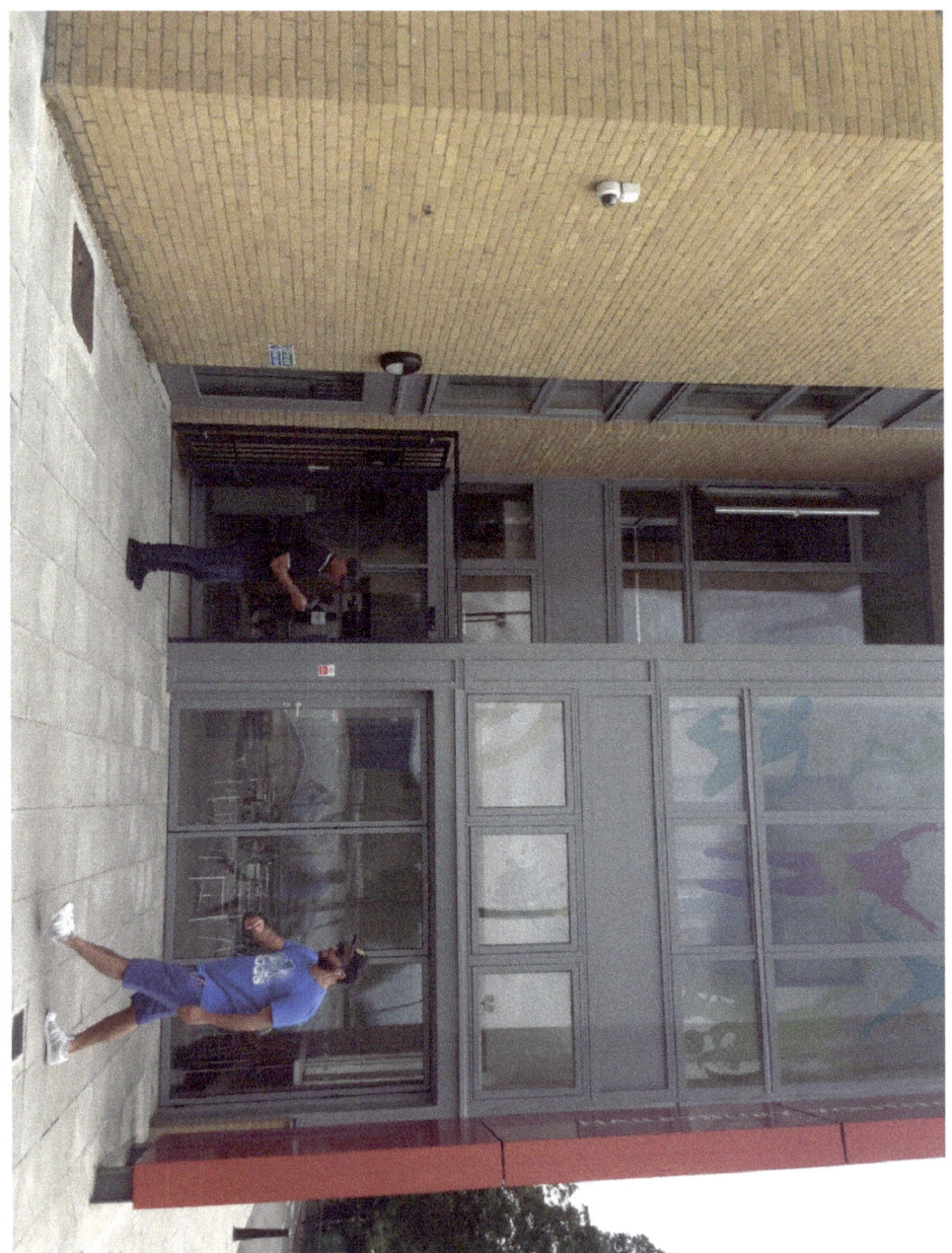

26.6.2016 - 14:45:12, Hailebury Center, Ben Johnson Road.

East End Photos, Through Mayar's Eyes : **Tower Hamlets, Random One**

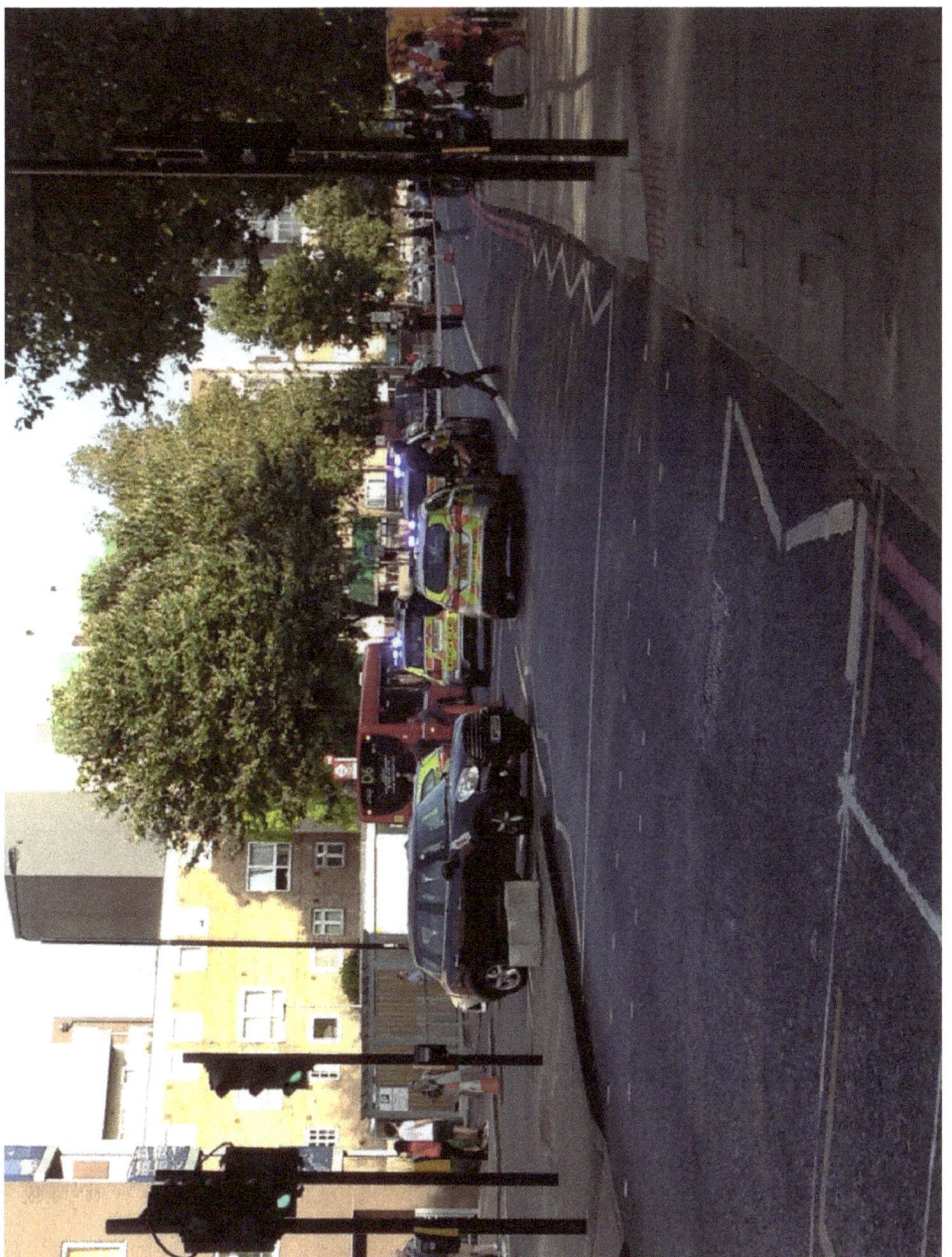

16.8.2016 - 17:57:17, Burdett Road, Incident

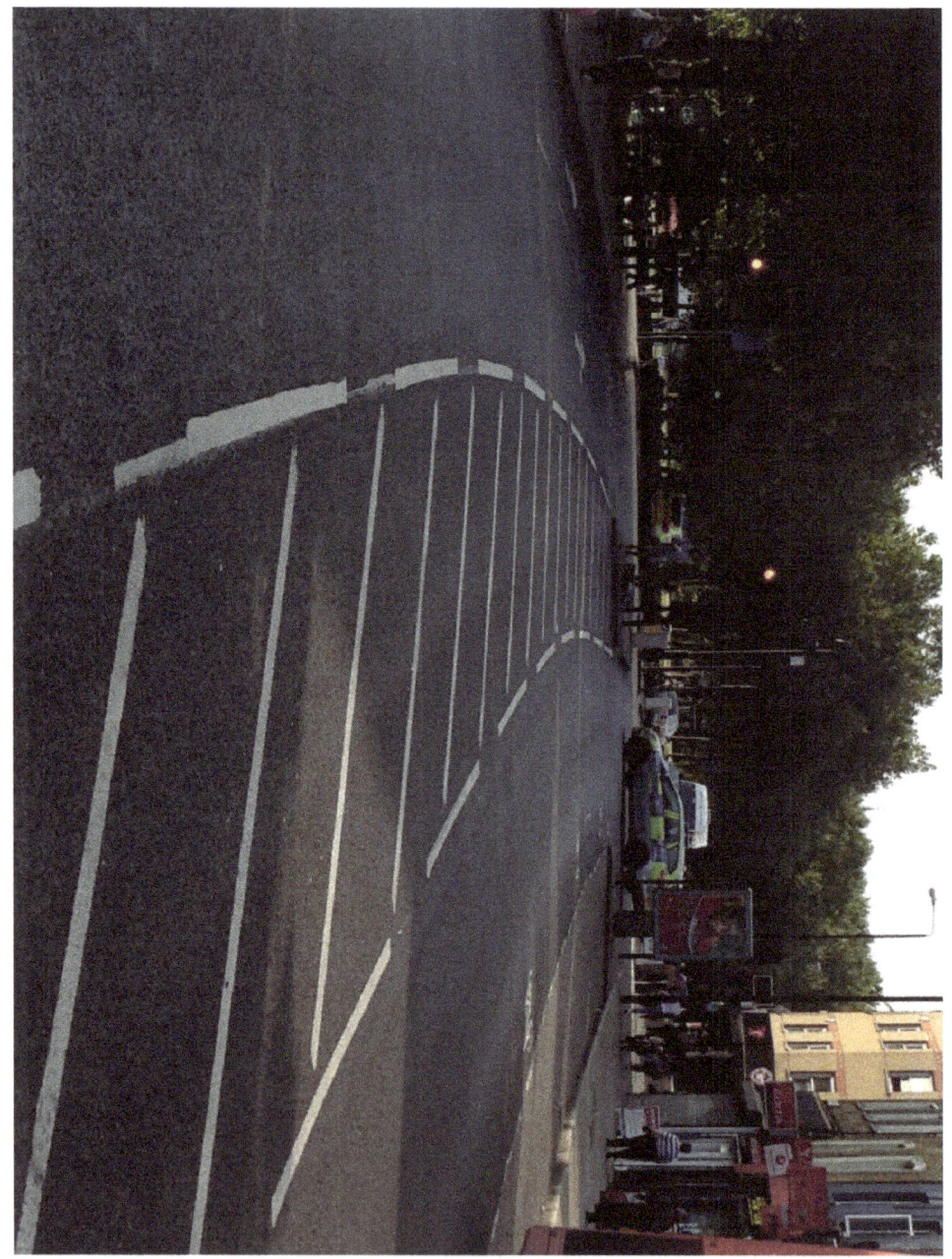

16.8.2016 - 17:57:27, Burdett Road, Incident, Road Closure

East End Photos, Through Mayar's Eyes : **Tower Hamlets, Random One**

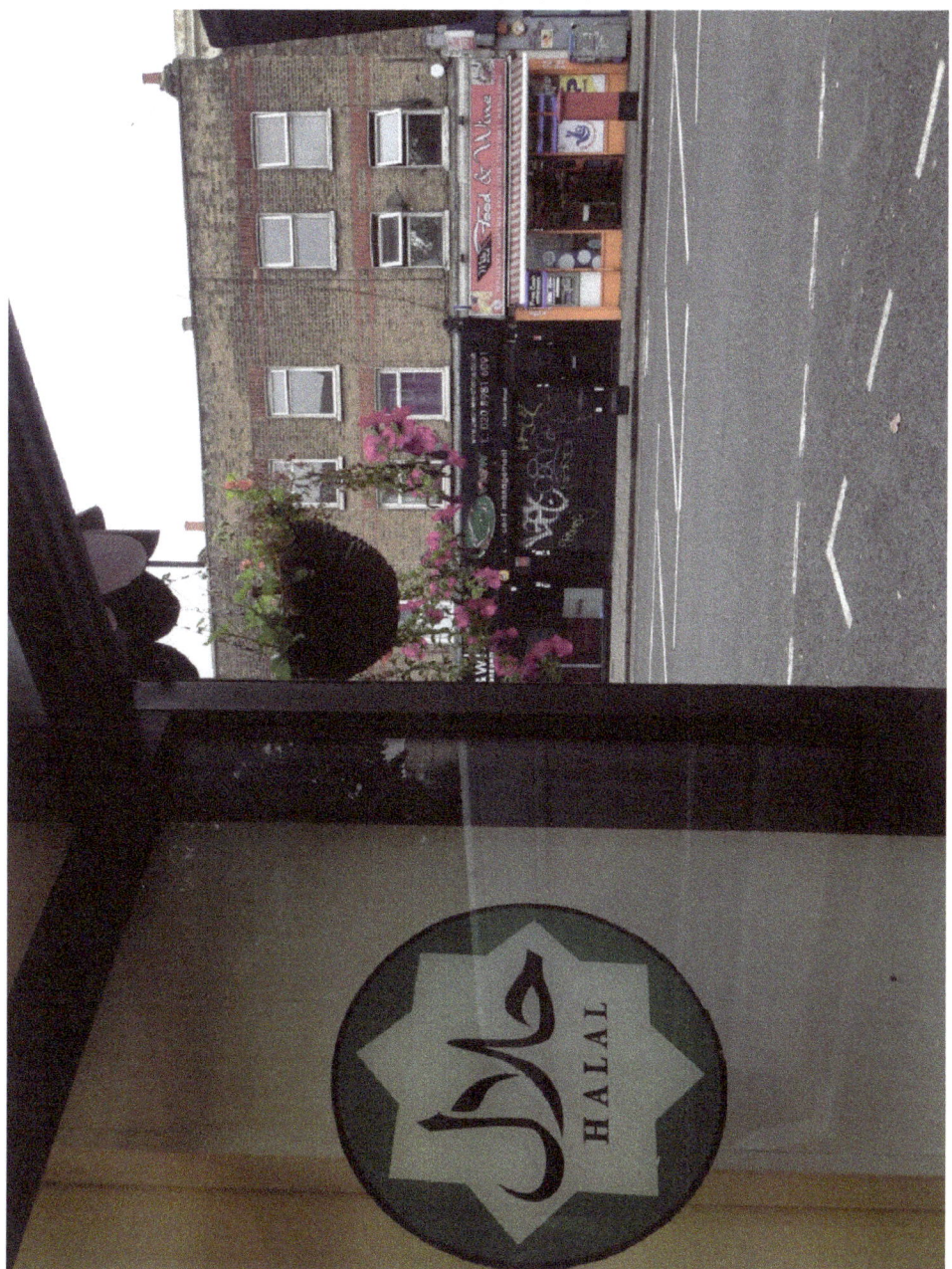

6.9.2016 - 14:11:26, Burdette Road, From Top Pizza shop, Lunch time

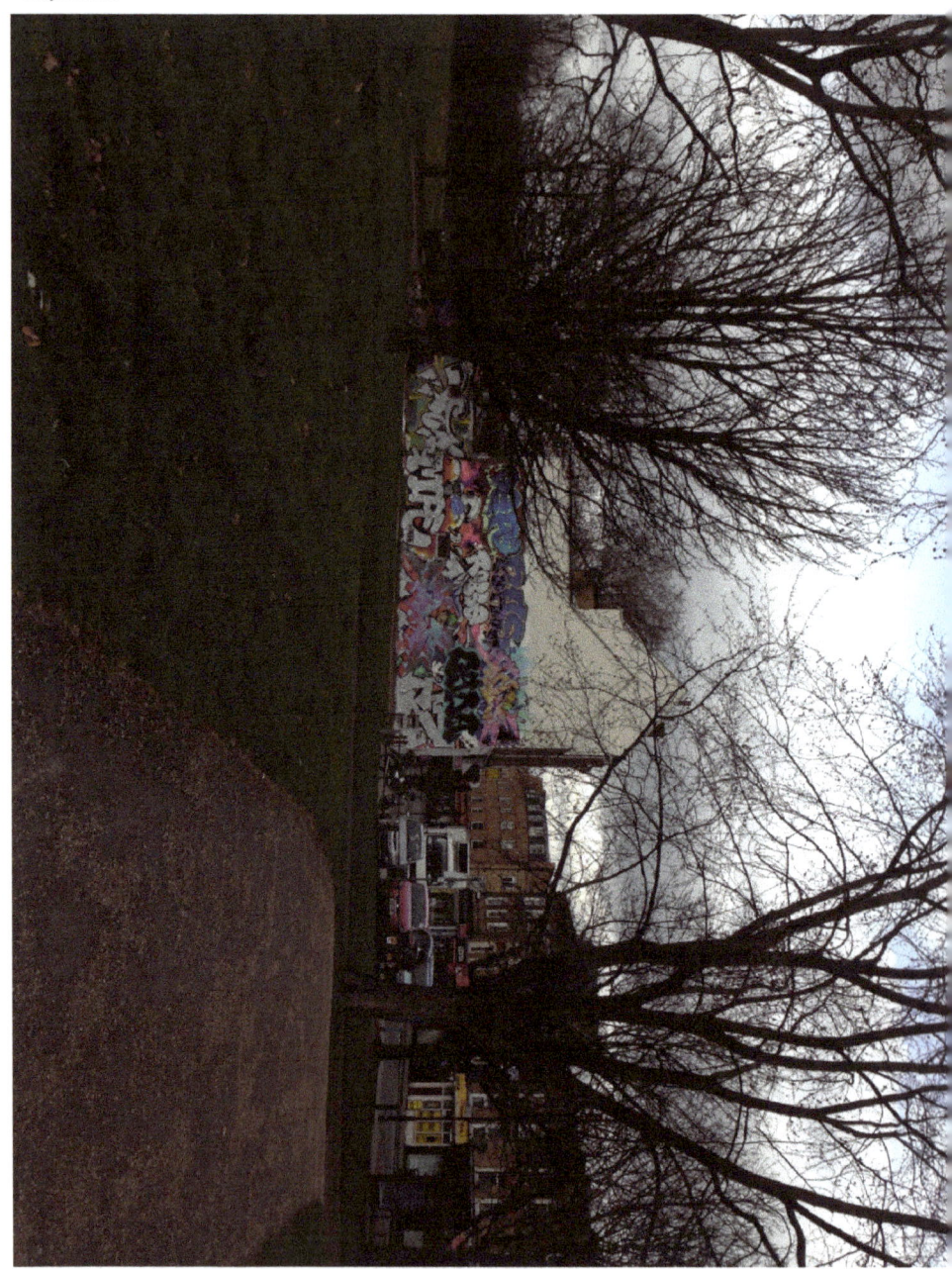

5.3.2015 - 14:59:08, Mile End Park, Burdett Road

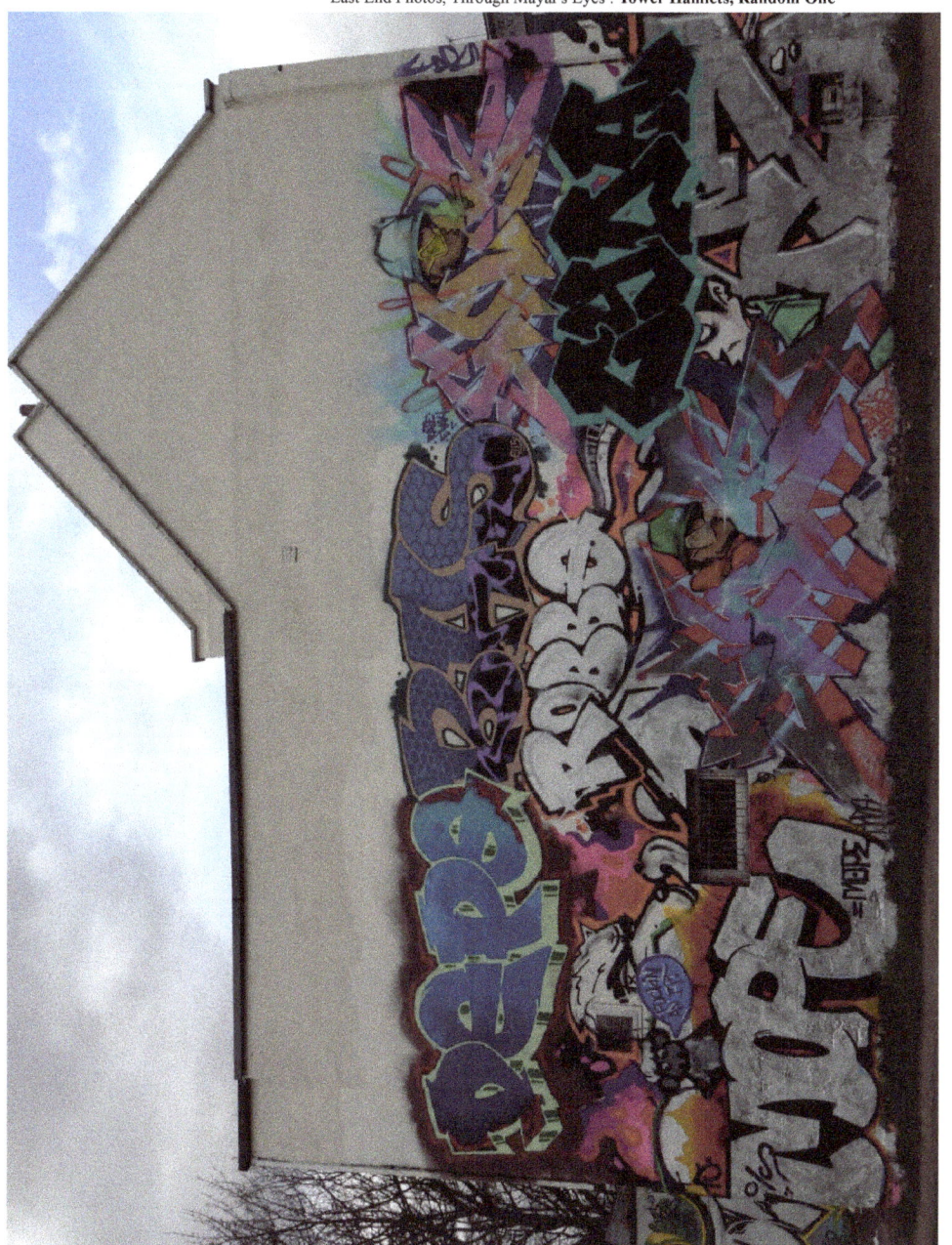

5.3.2015 - 14:59:53, Tops Pizza Restaurant Building, Mile End Park, Burdett road

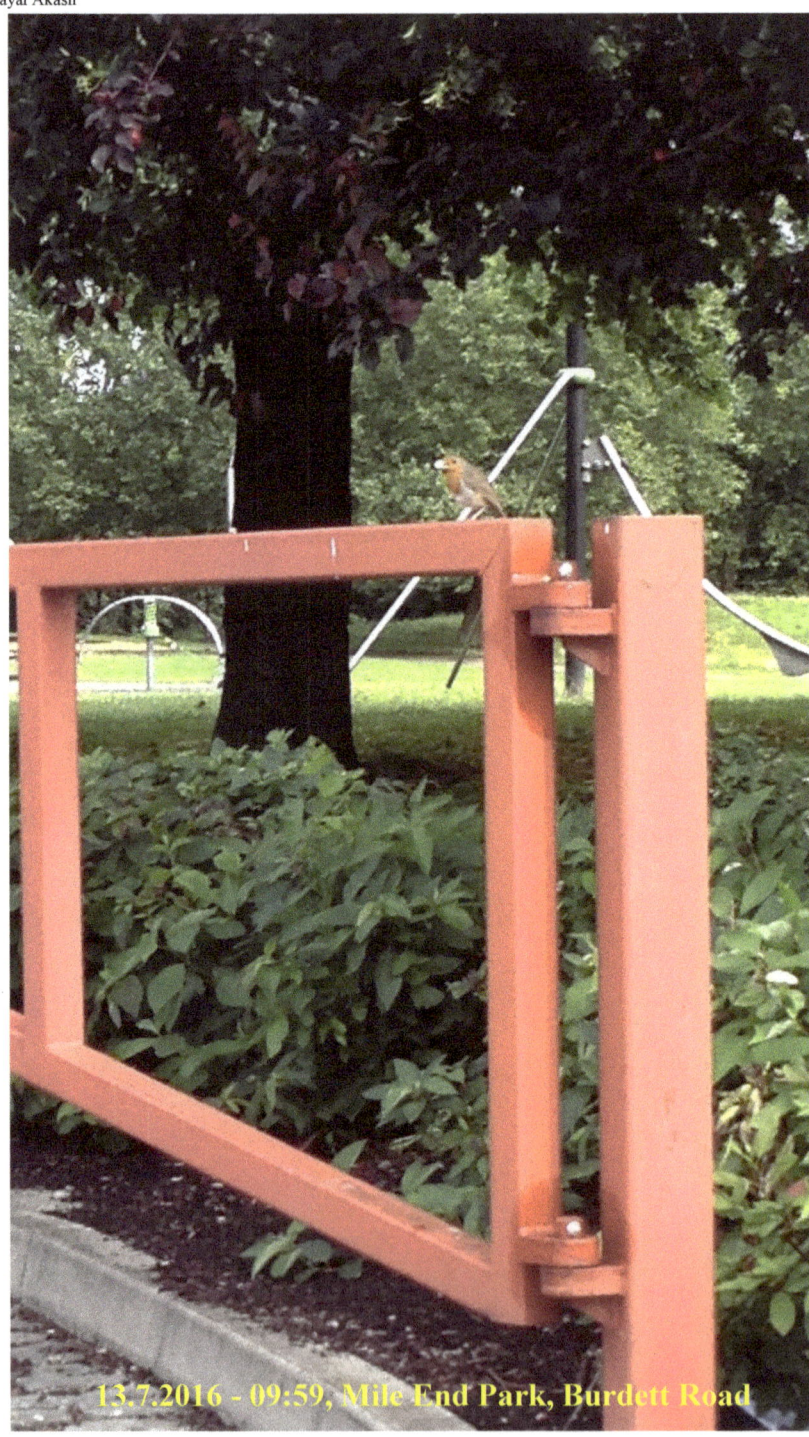

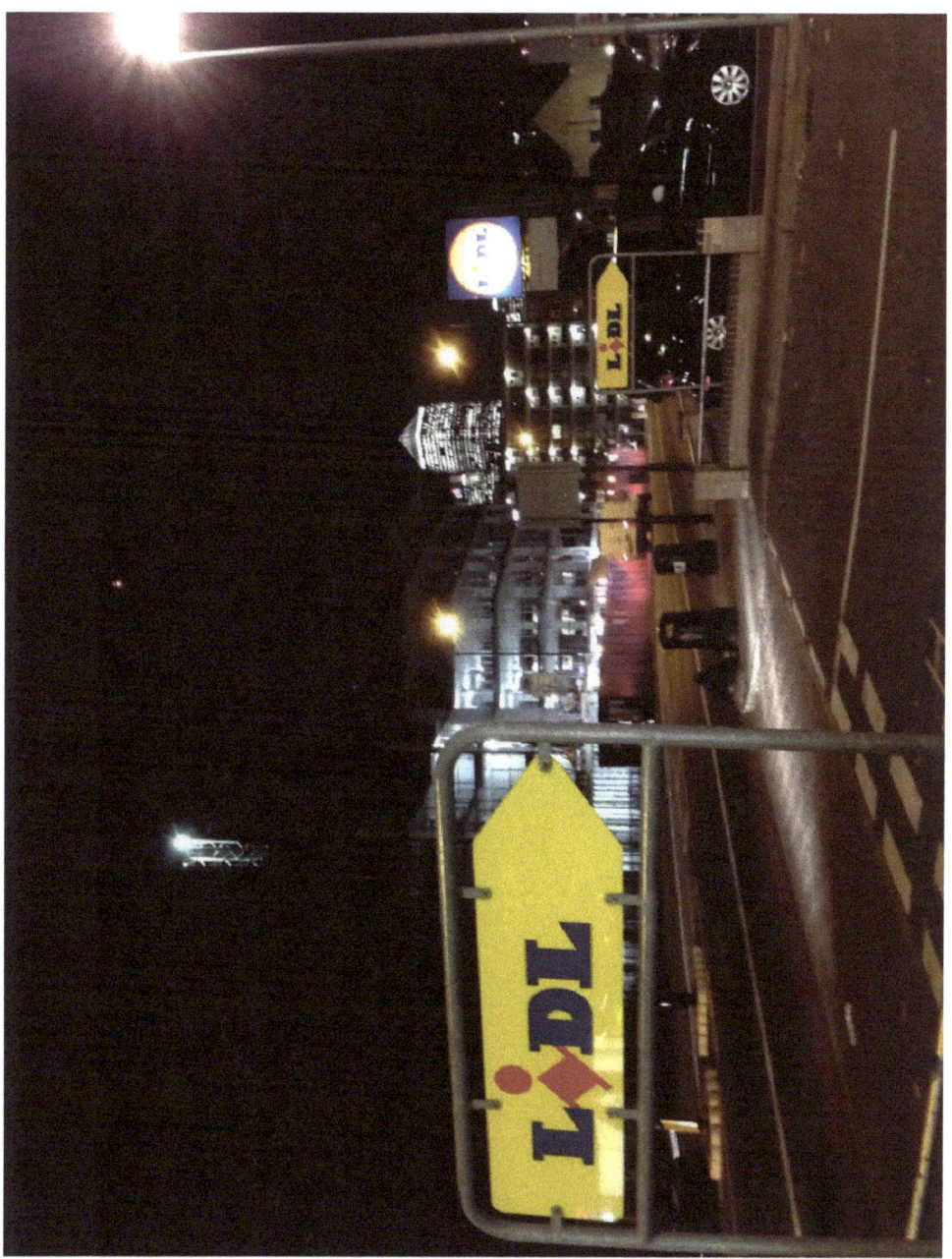

2.11.2016 - 18:19:, Lidl Car park, Burdett Road.

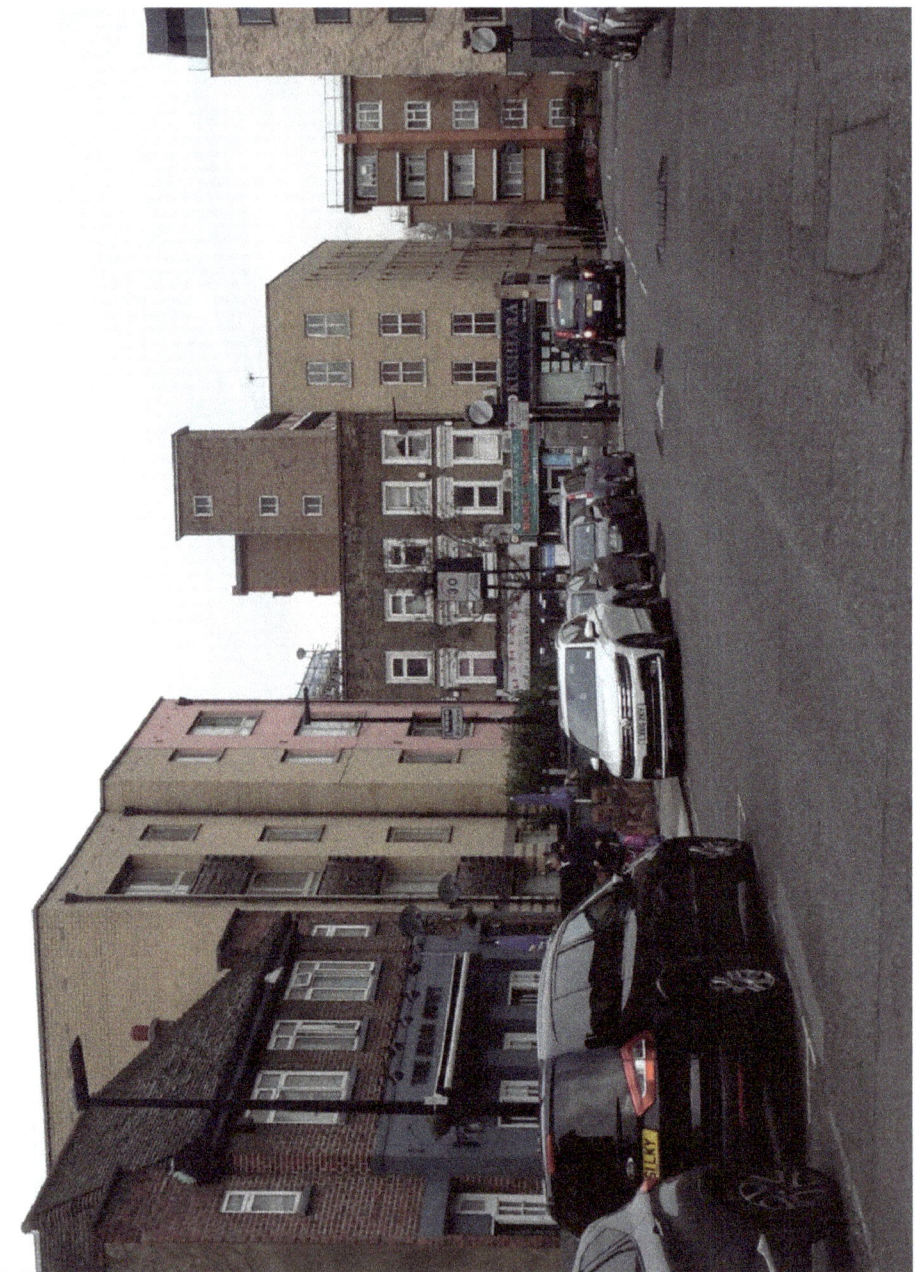

6.2.2017 - 13:02:14, Deancross Street, off Commercial Road

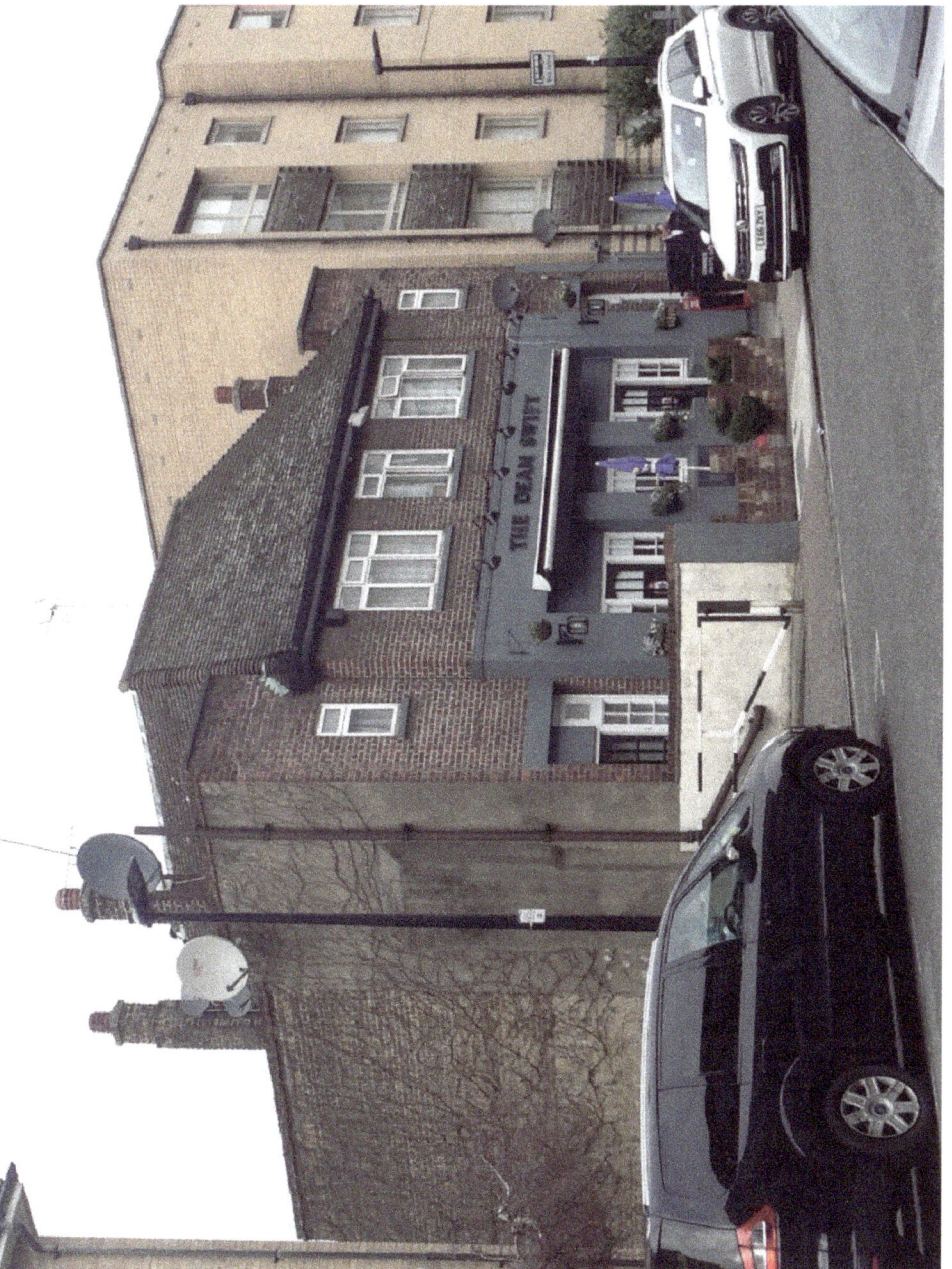

6.2.2017 - Deancross Street Pub

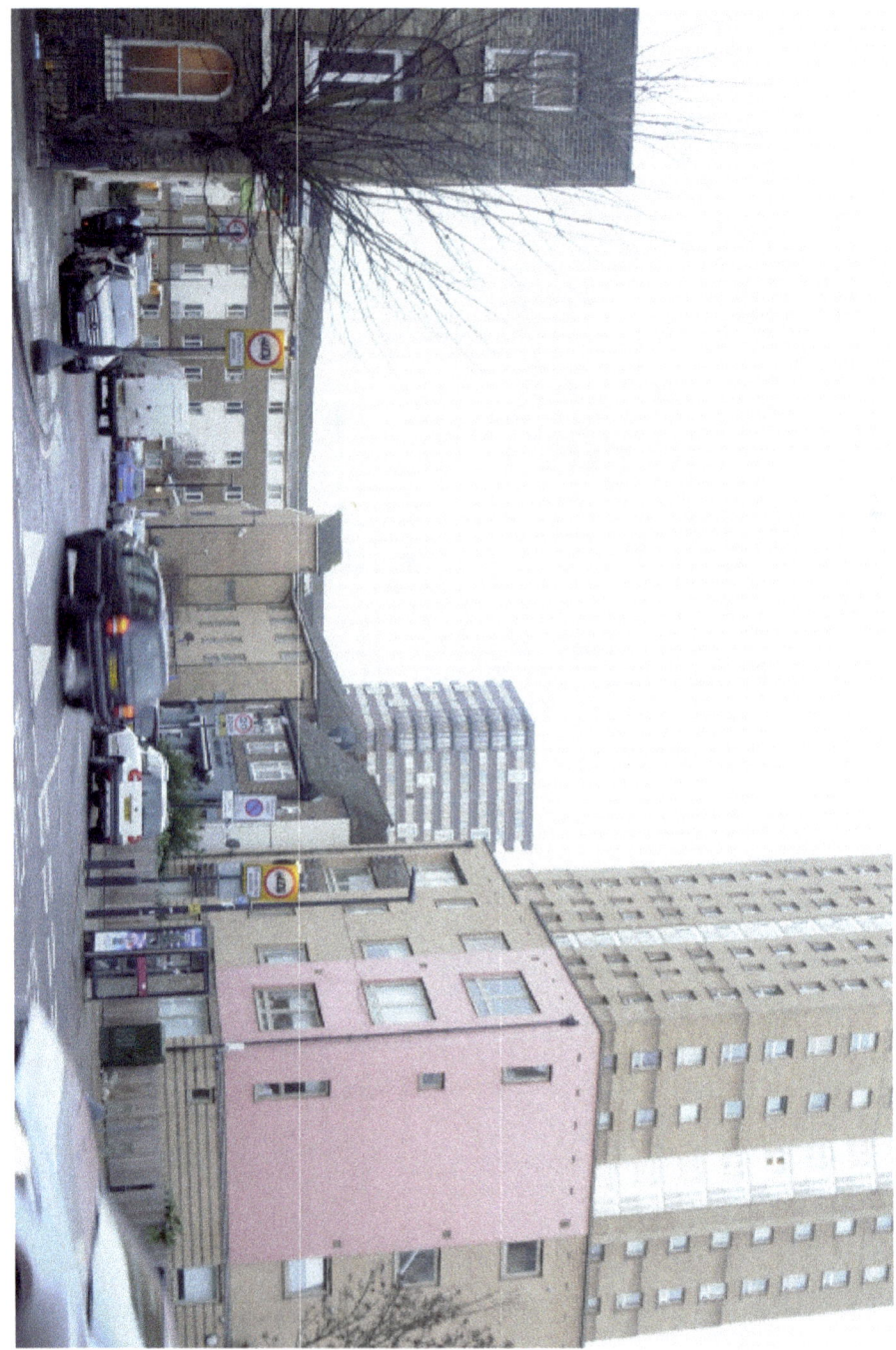

14.1.2017 - 17:01:12, View from Commercial Road

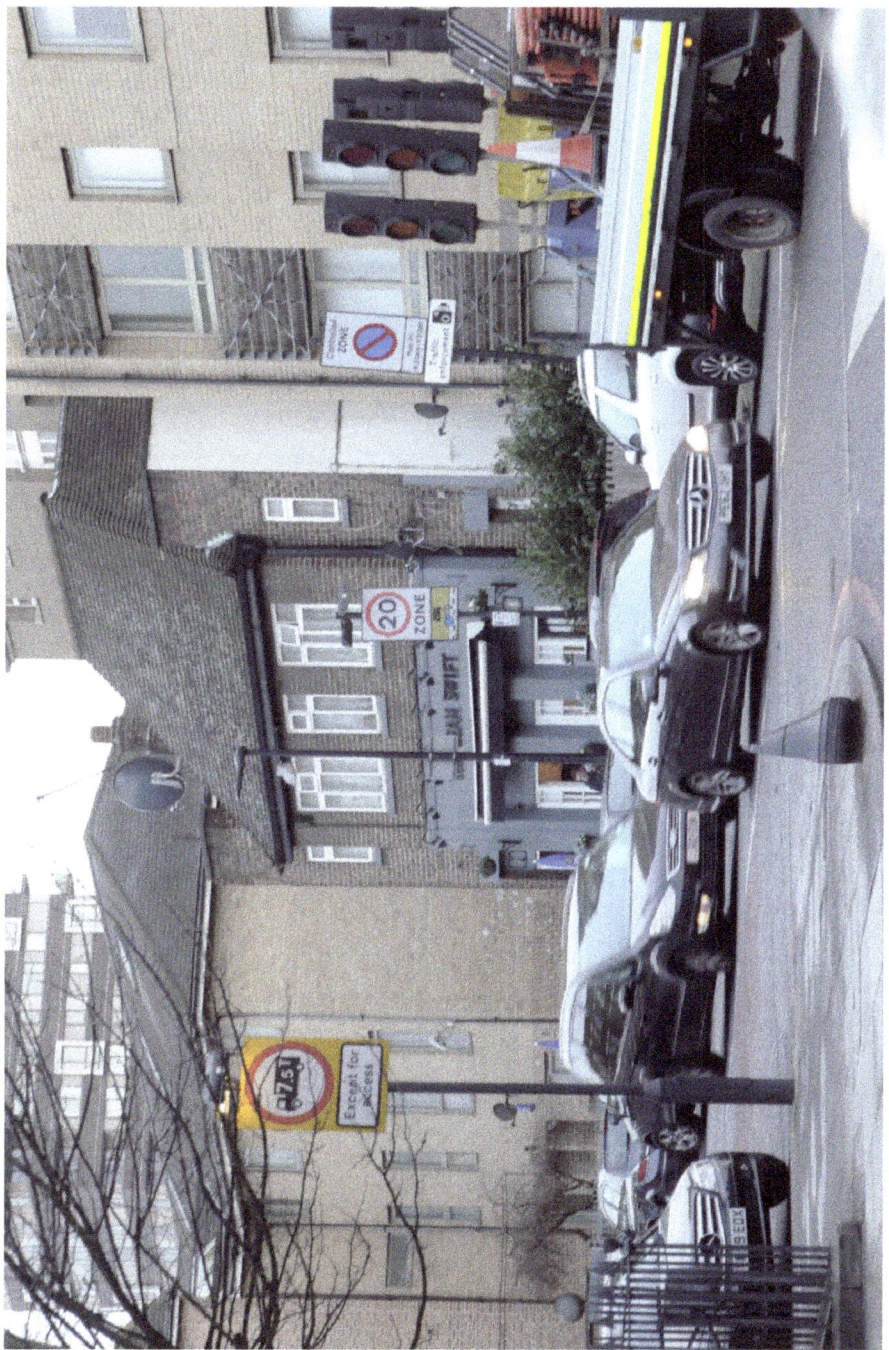

14-1.2017 - 17:02:52, The Dean Swift Pub

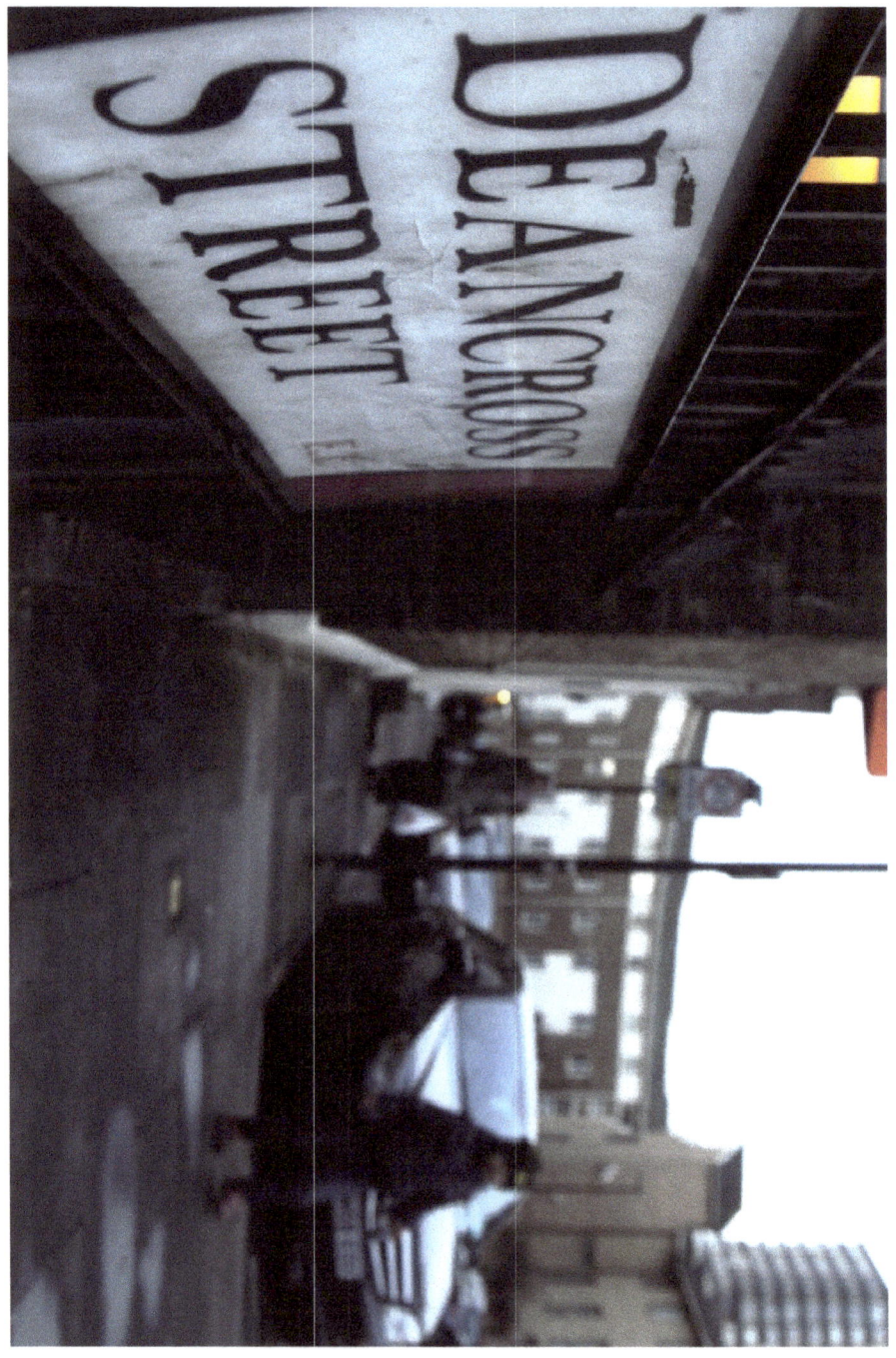

14.1.2017 - 17:03:46,

East End Photos, Through Mayar's Eyes : **Tower Hamlets, Random One**

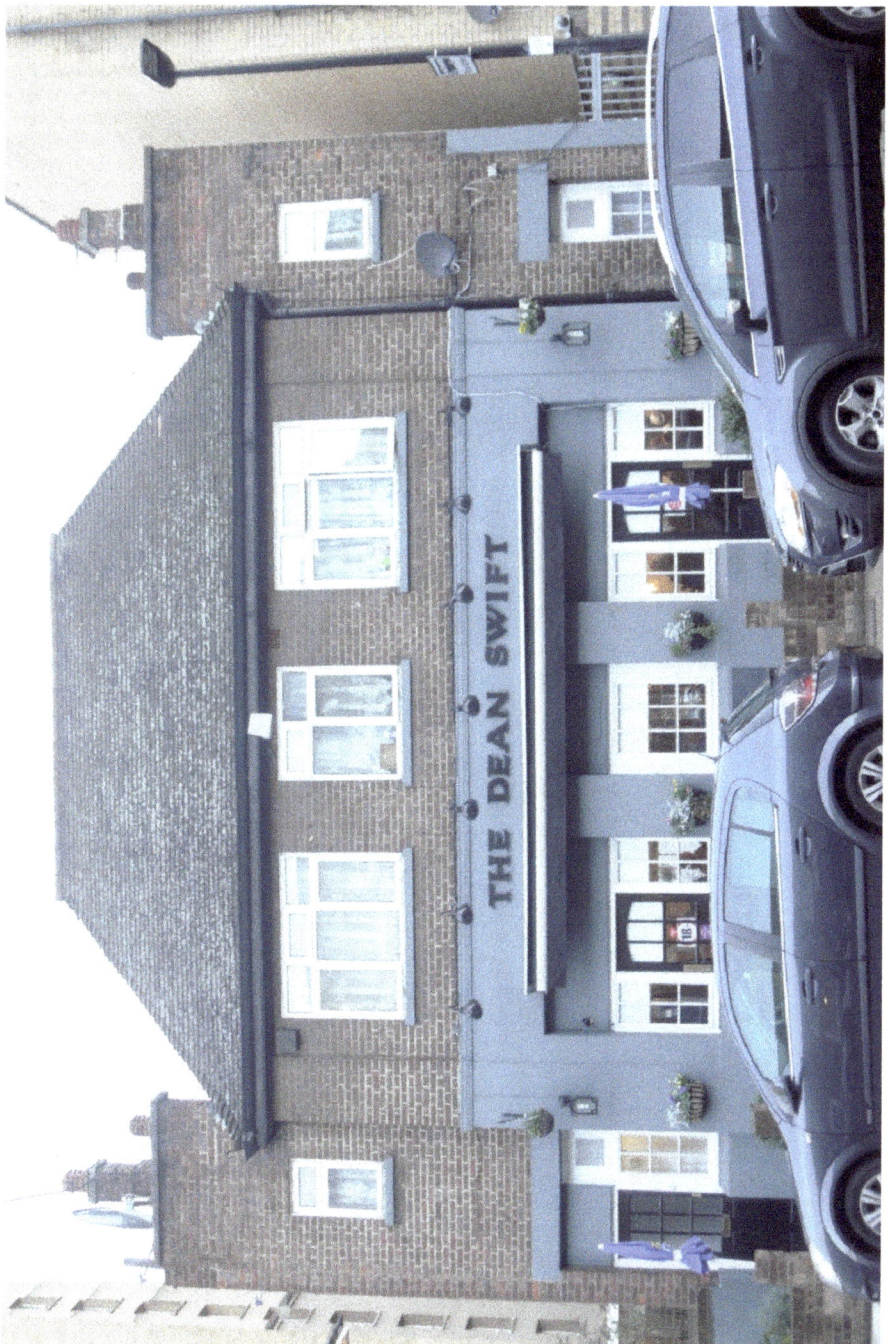

14.1.2017 - 17:04:38

Mayar Akash

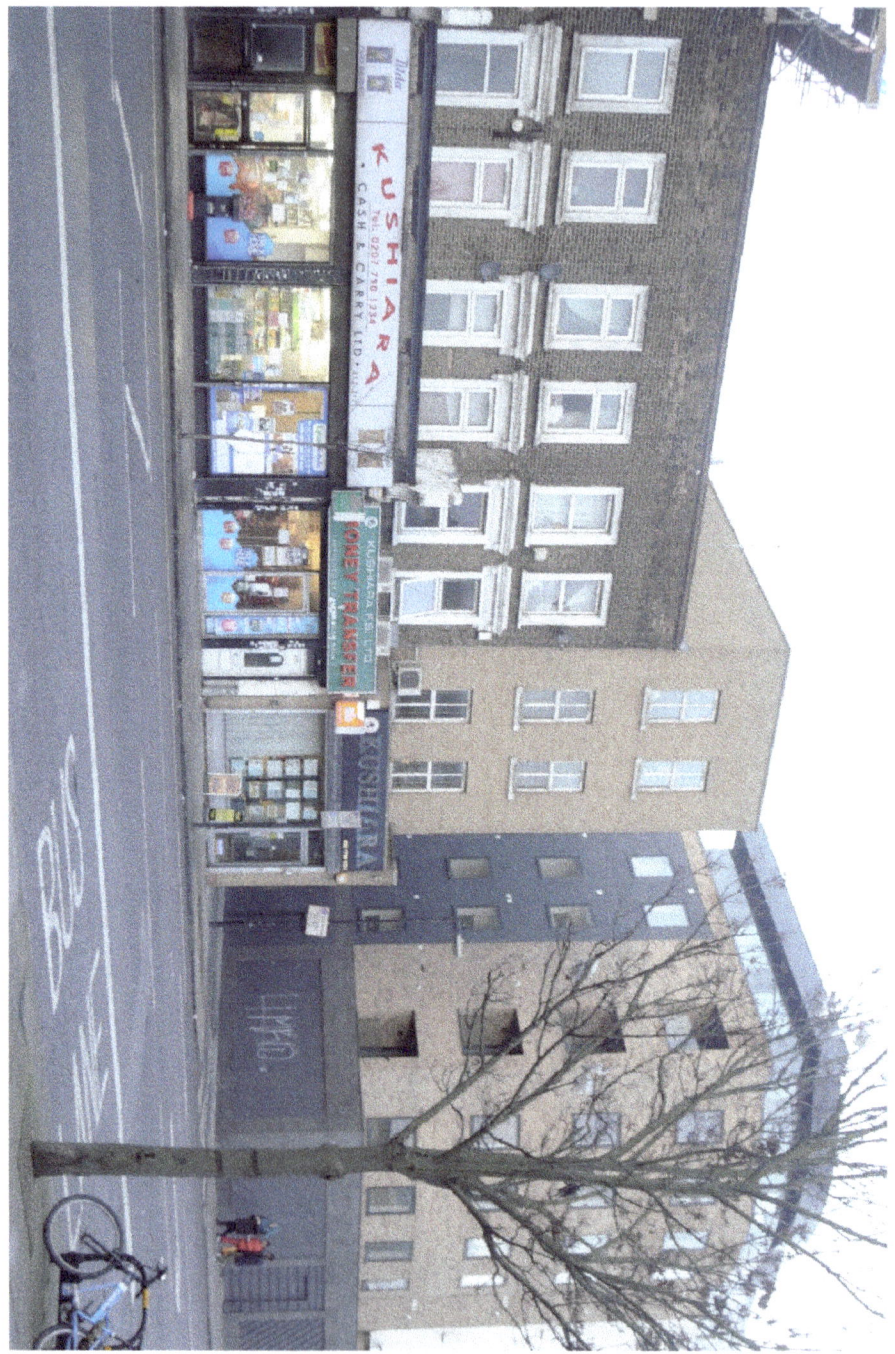

14.1.2017 - 17:06:50, Kushiara Shops, On Commercial Road

East End Photos, Through Mayar's Eyes : **Tower Hamlets, Random One**

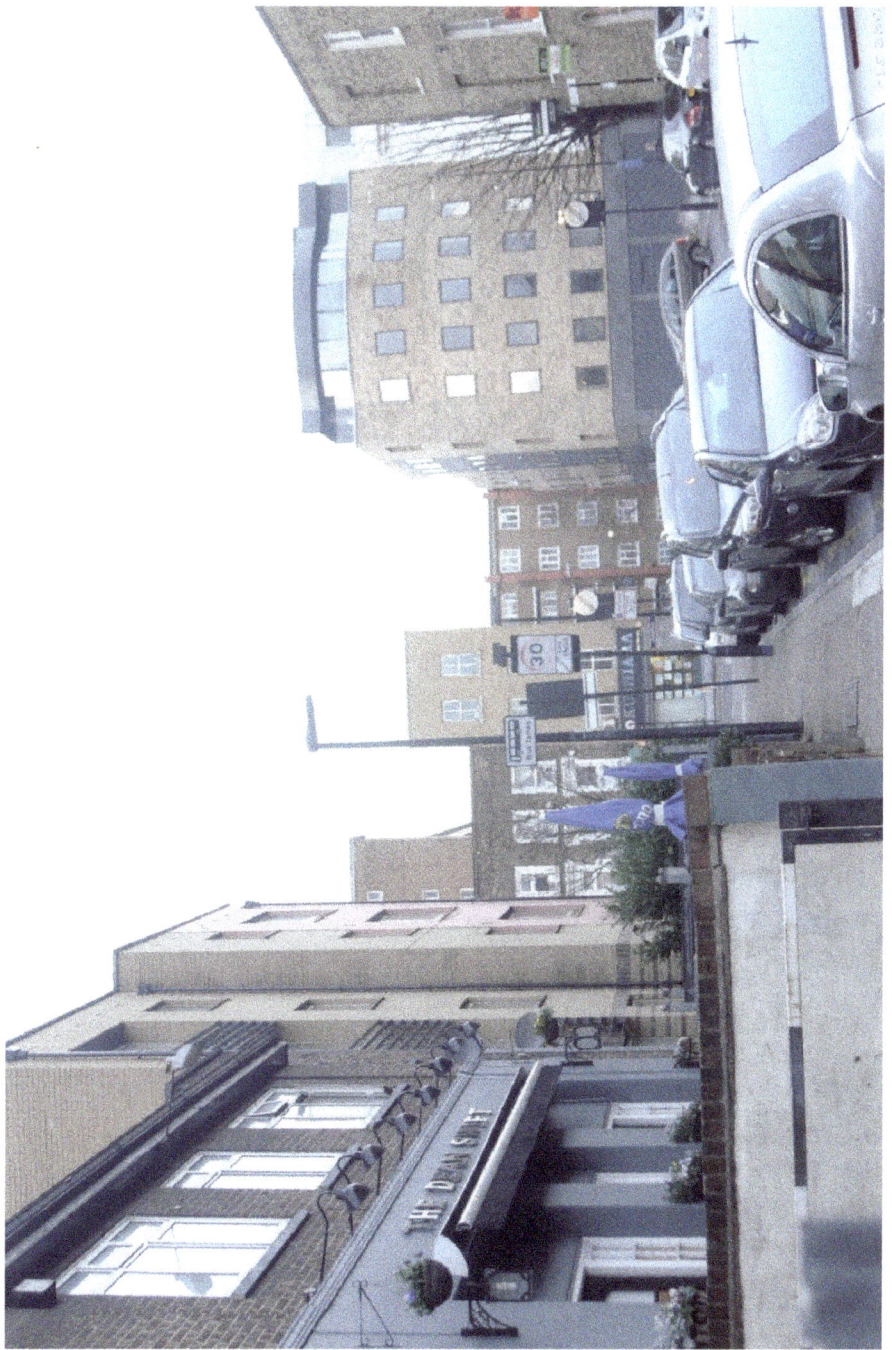

14.1.2017 - 17:05:06, Kushiara Building from Deancross Street

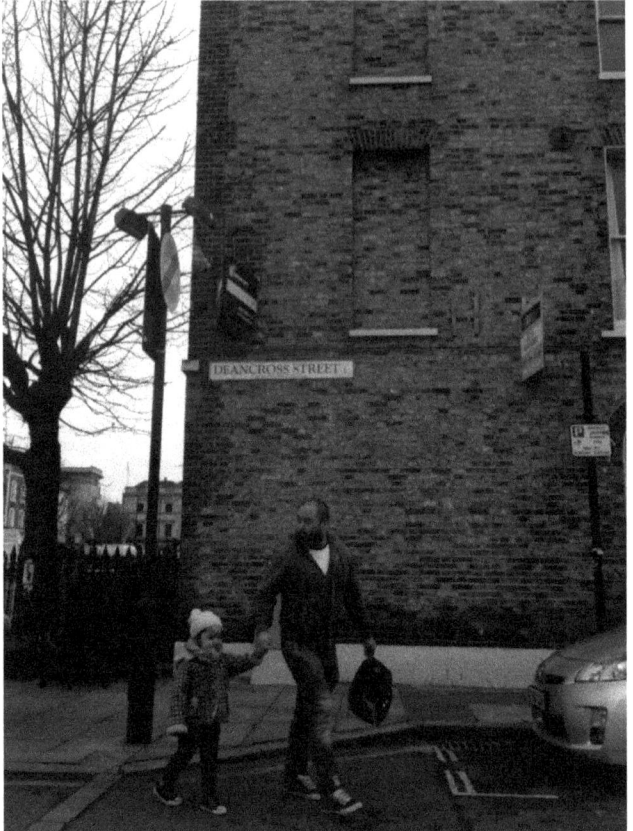

6.2.2017 - 13:03:

Deancross street, came into my conscience after many years, it was something I was going to do but went off the radar.

Quddus Ali was attacked on the corner of this road, opposite side of the picture.

Adults drinking in the pub, (The Dean Swift) that day, beat him up and left him to die. he survived but severely disabled.

All this happened during the by-election time in Millwall, where Dereck Beackon was contesting.

> I was there at the vigil at Whitechapel Road, London Hospital, yet I never got round to this place. So a belated homage to him and his ordeal.

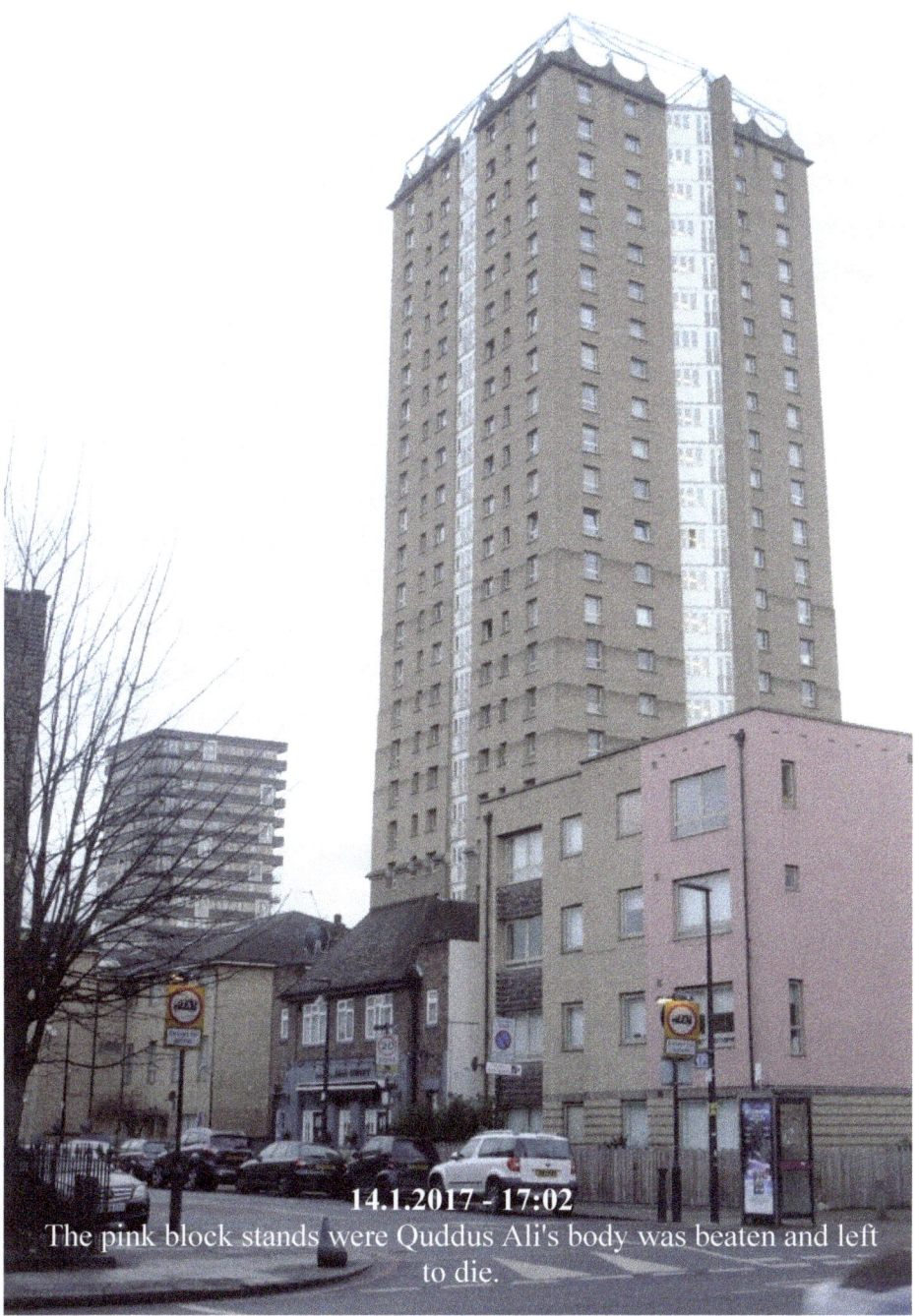

14.1.2017 - 17:02
The pink block stands were Quddus Ali's body was beaten and left to die.

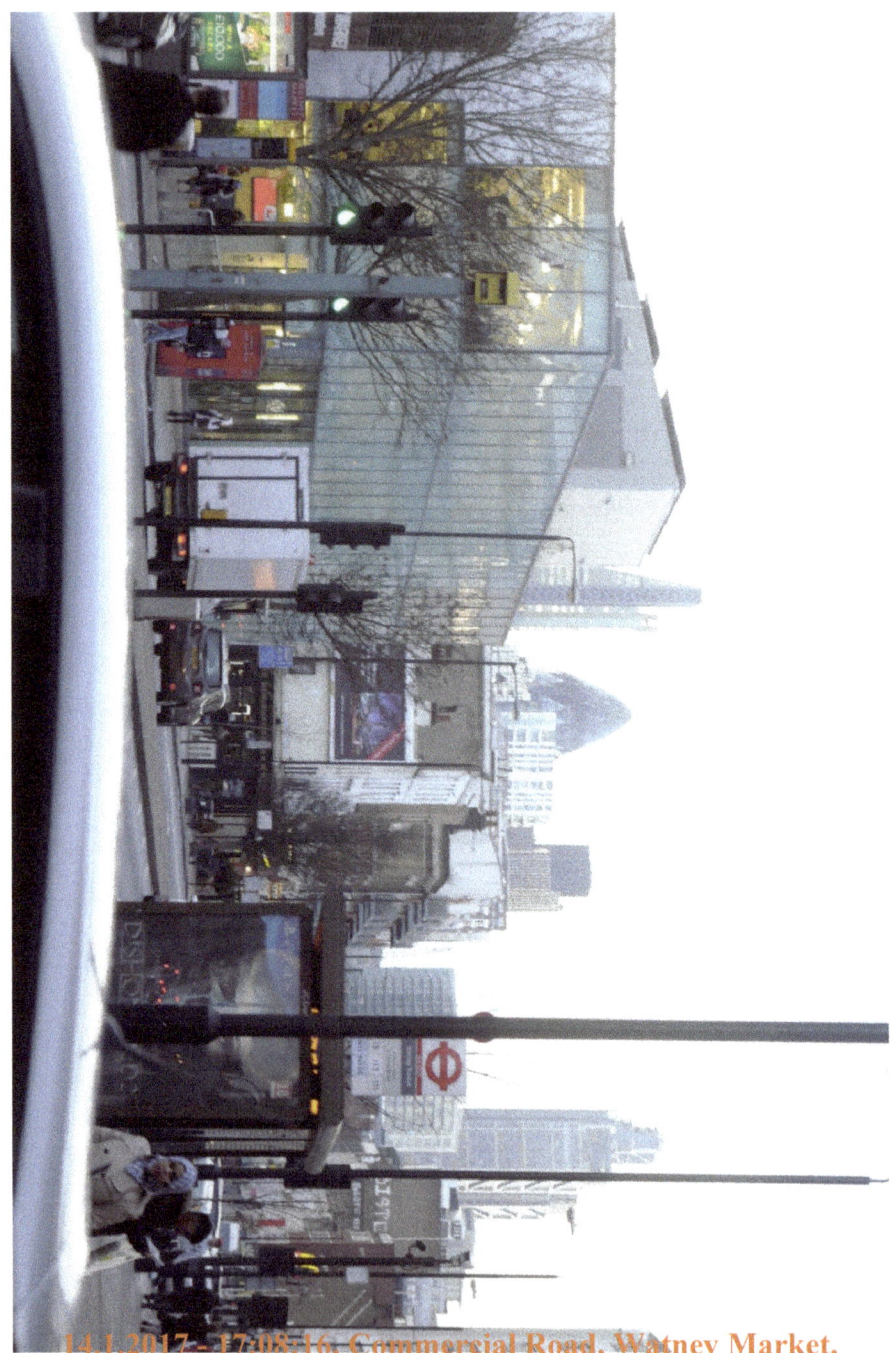

14.1.2017 – 17:08:16, Commercial Road, Watney Market, towards Aldgate

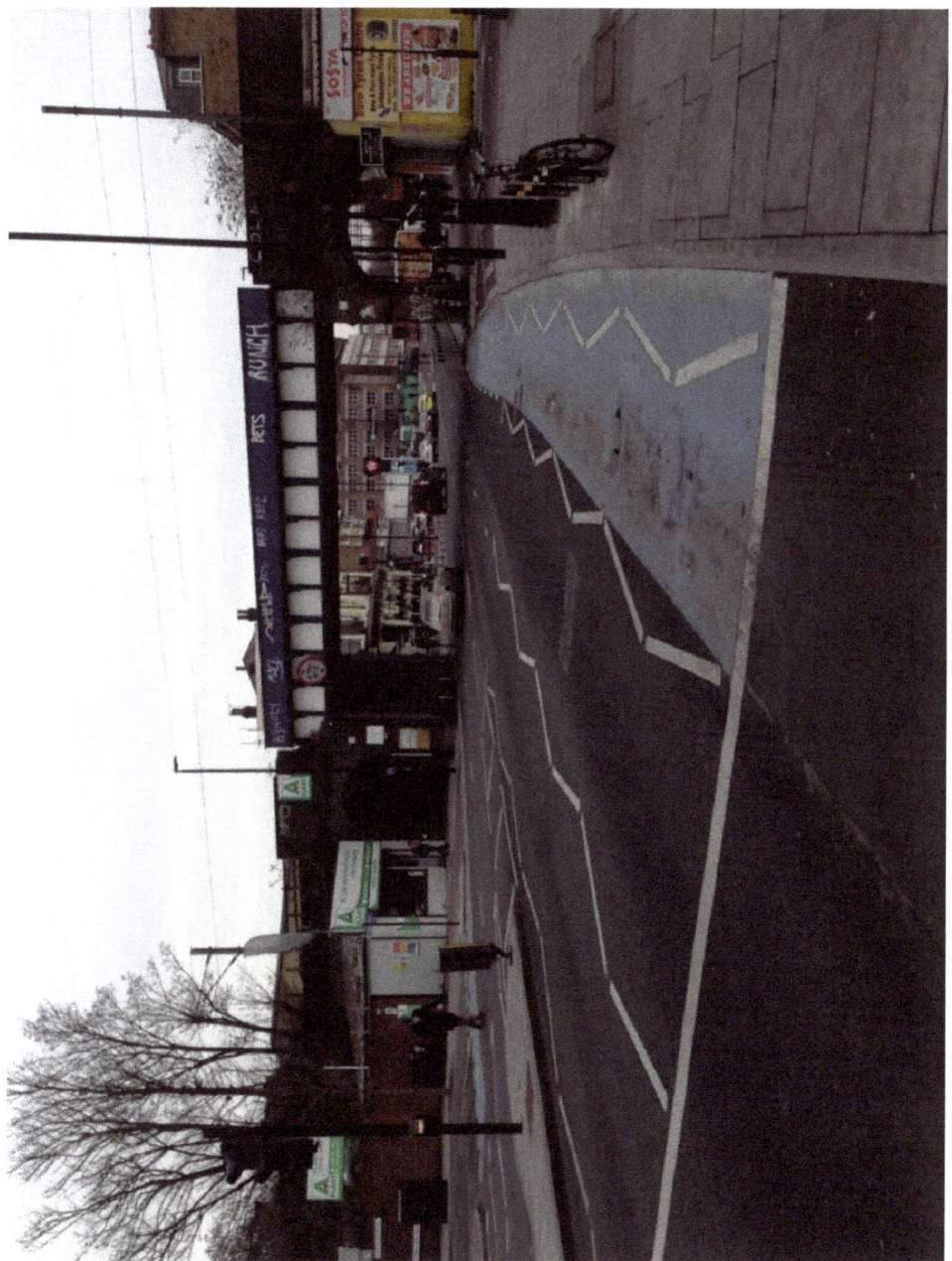

6.2.2017 - 13:25:10, Bow Road, Outside the Thames Magistrate Court

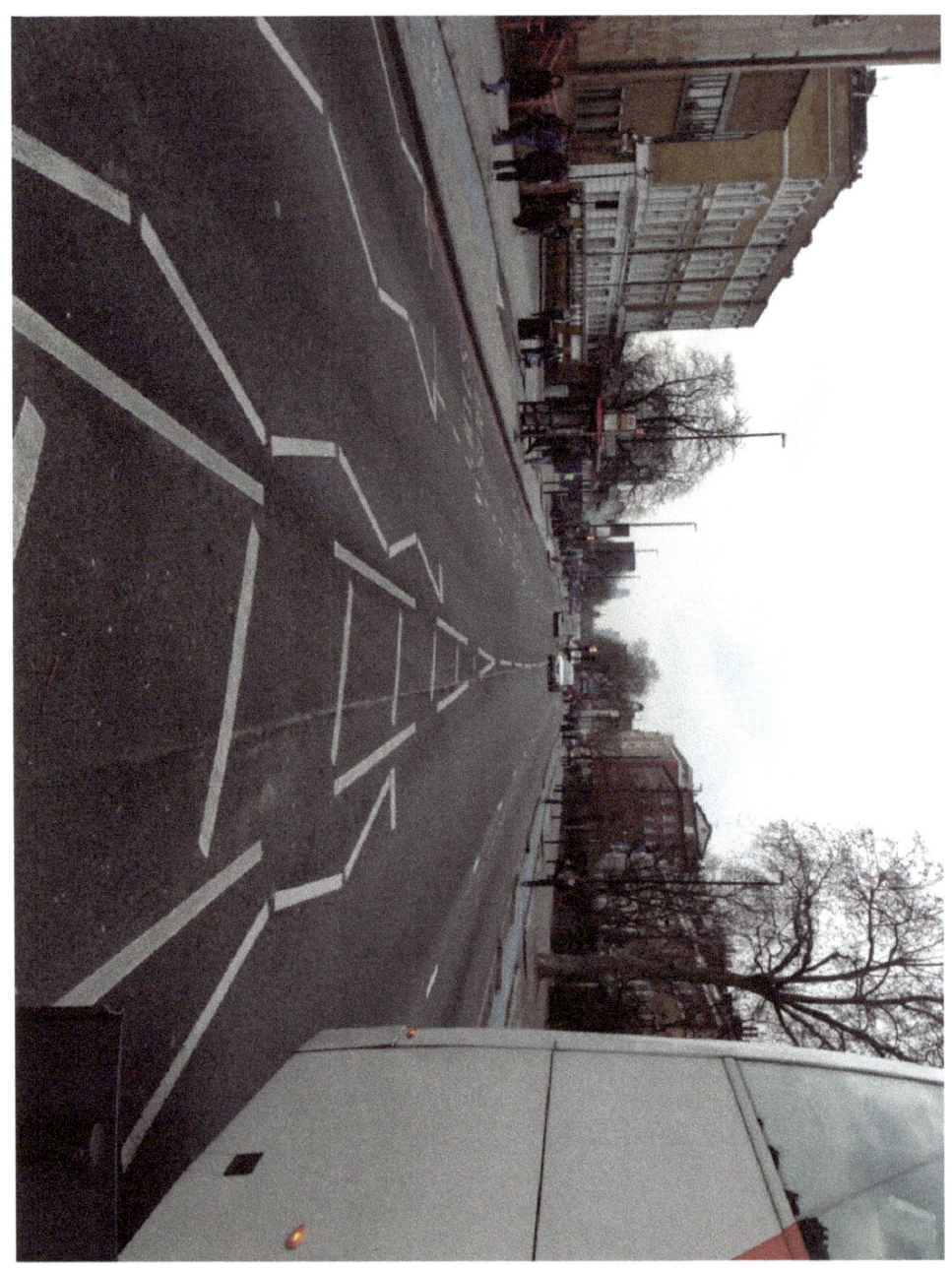

6.2.2017 - 13:25:30, Bow Road,

East End Photos, Through Mayar's Eyes : **Tower Hamlets, Random One**

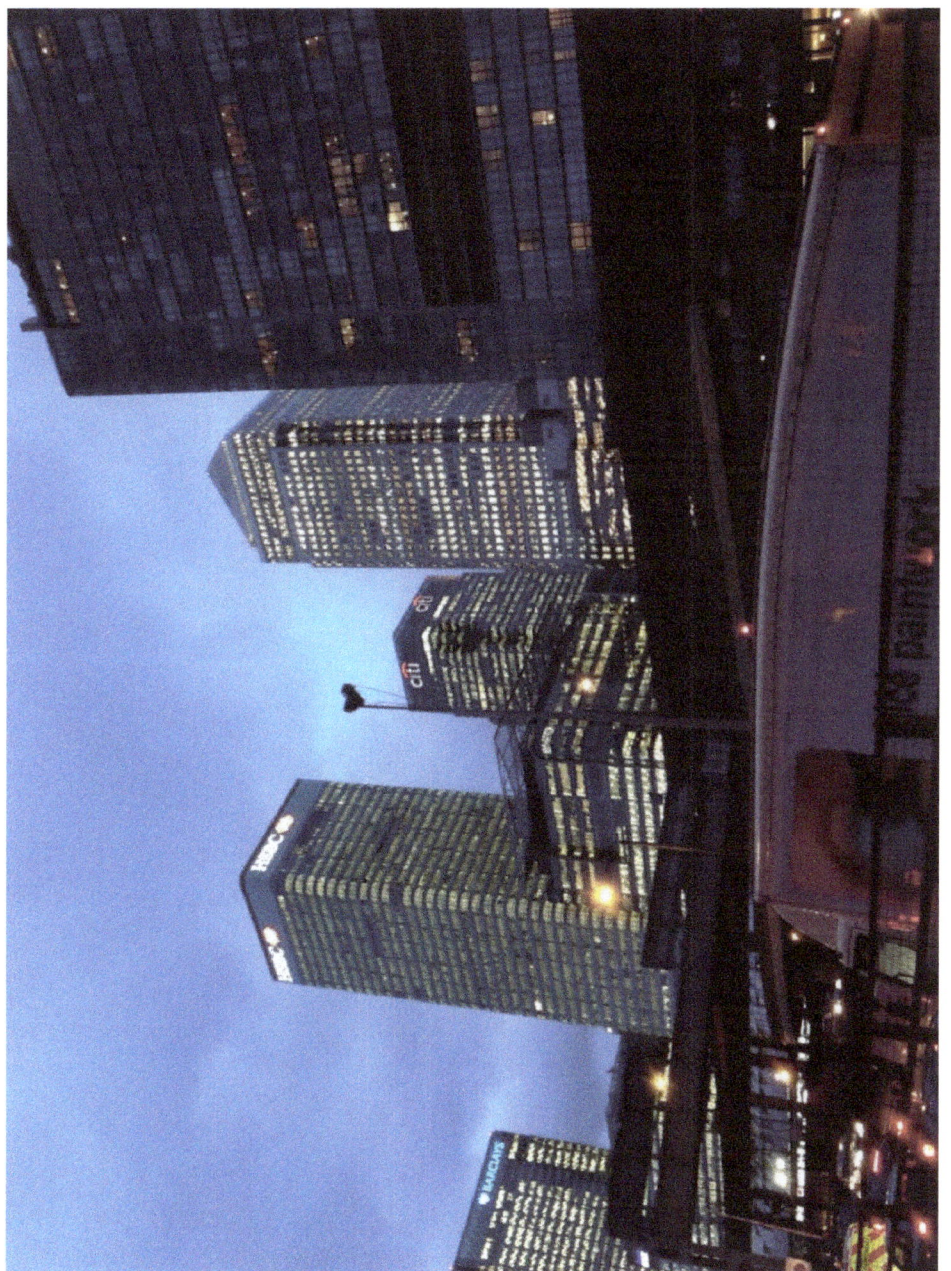

22.2.2017 - 17:41:44

Mayar Akash

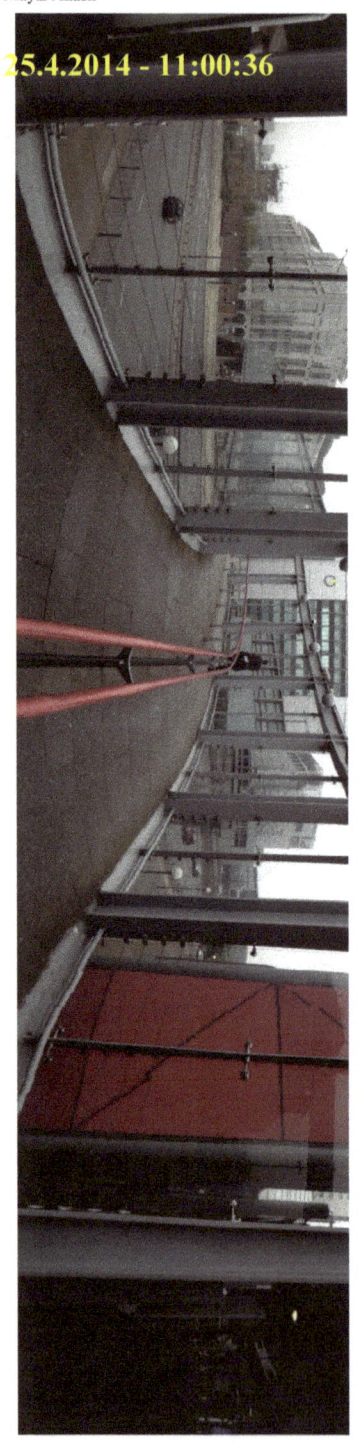

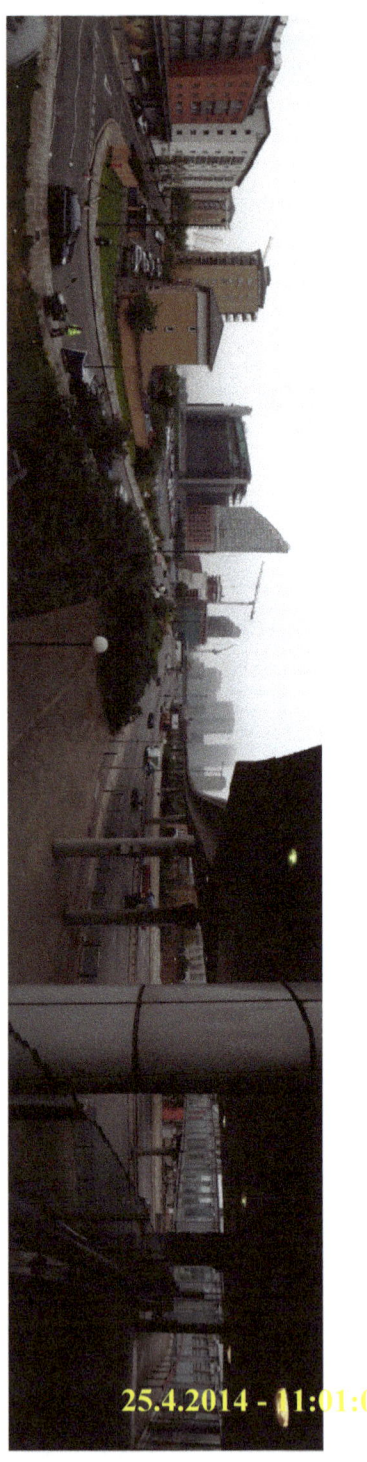

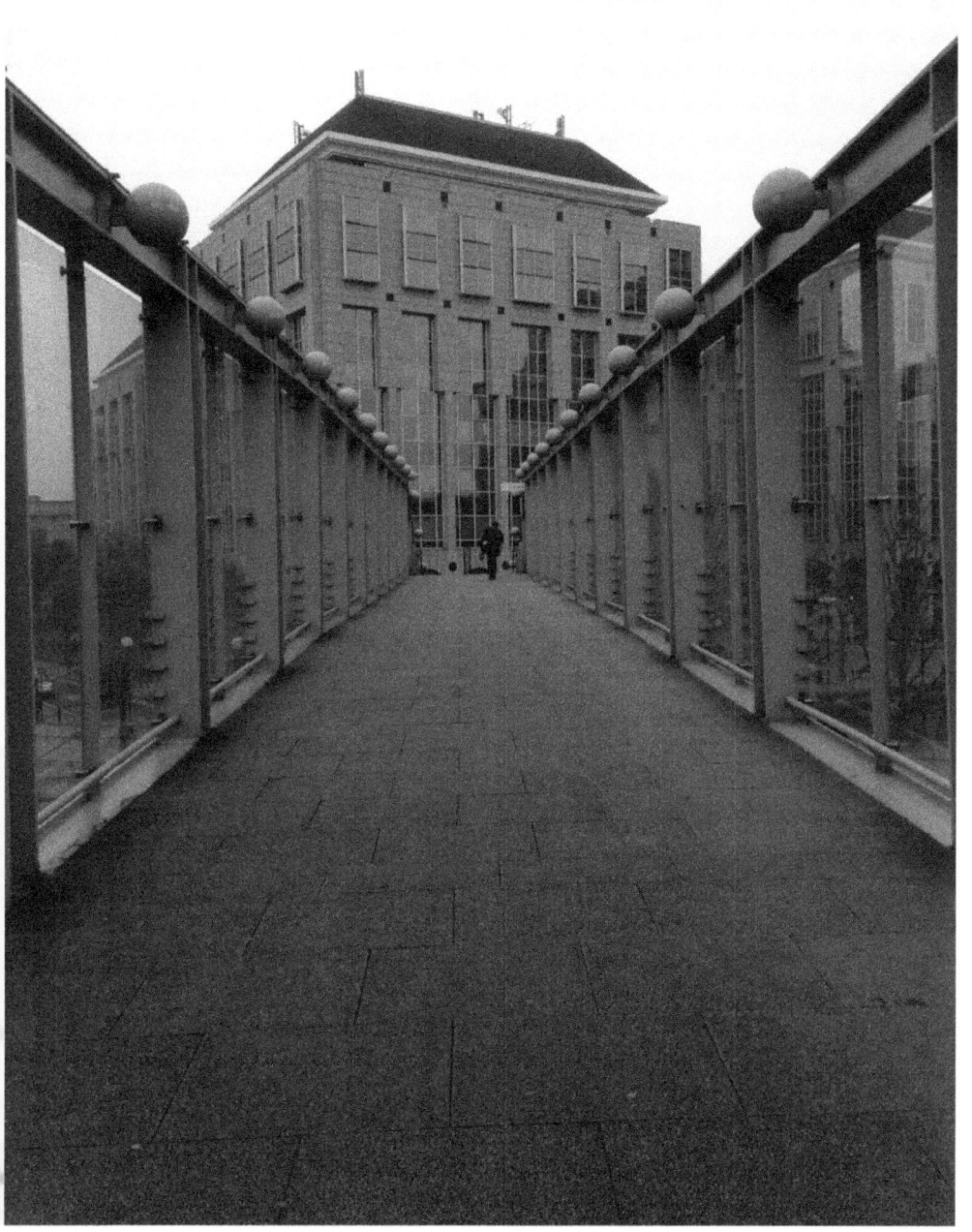

25.4.2014 - 11:01:28, Footbridge To Town Hall

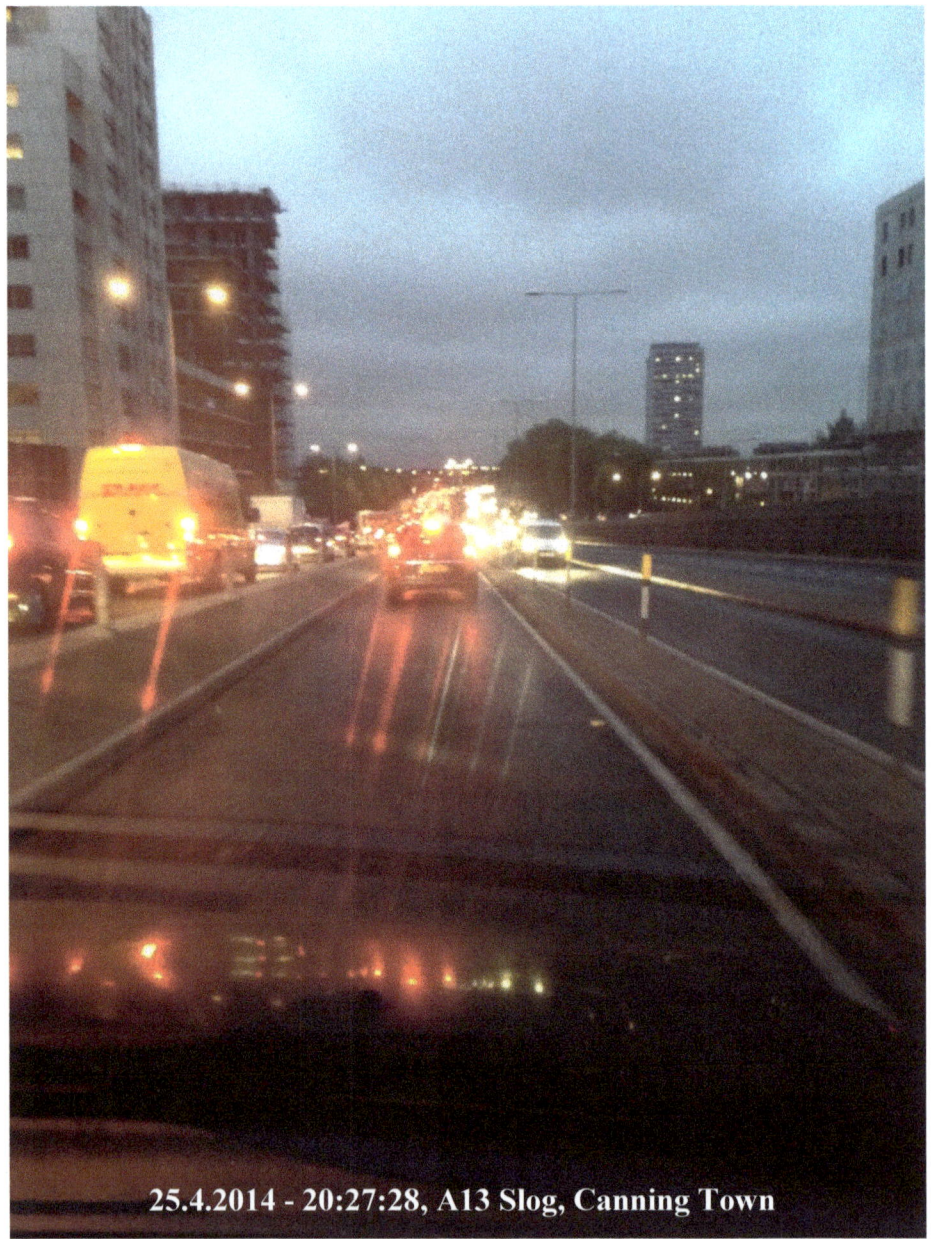

This became a routine for couple of years, stationary over the Canning Town flyer.

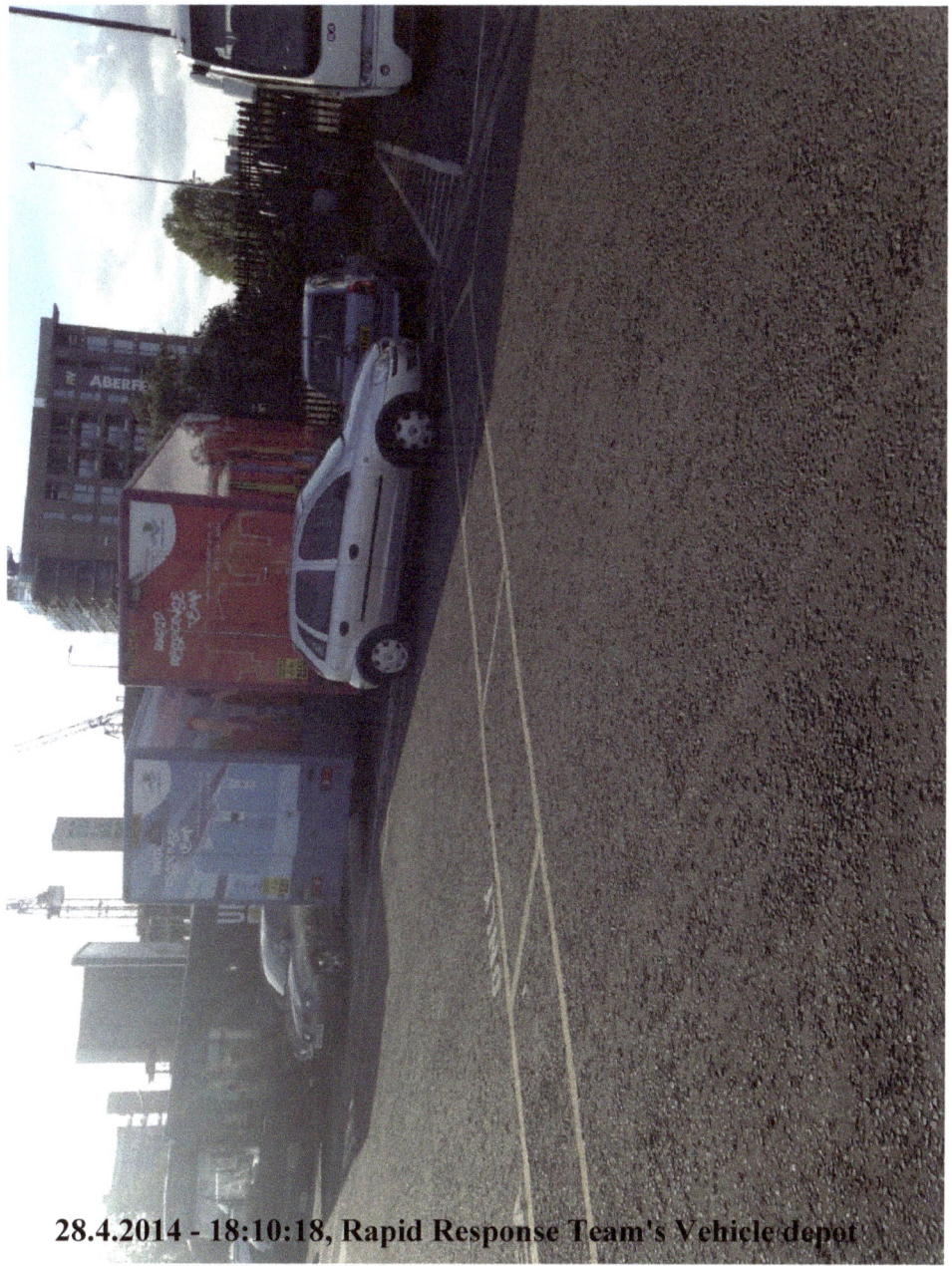

28.4.2014 - 18:10:18, Rapid Response Team's Vehicle depot

I was a driver for the Tower Hamlets RRT, driving those 7.5tonners.

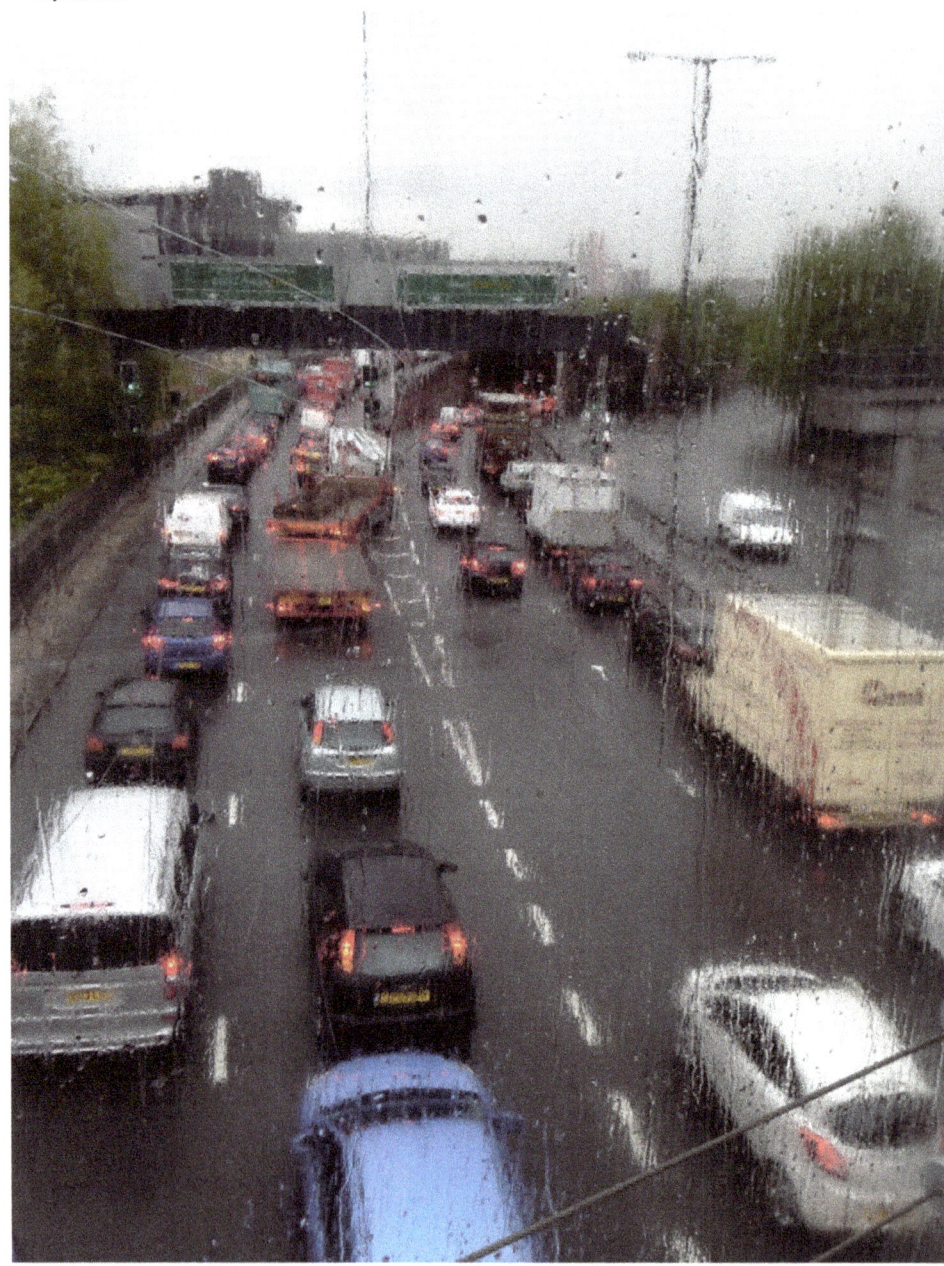

1.5.2014 - 18:16:45, Canning Town underpass, from foot bridge

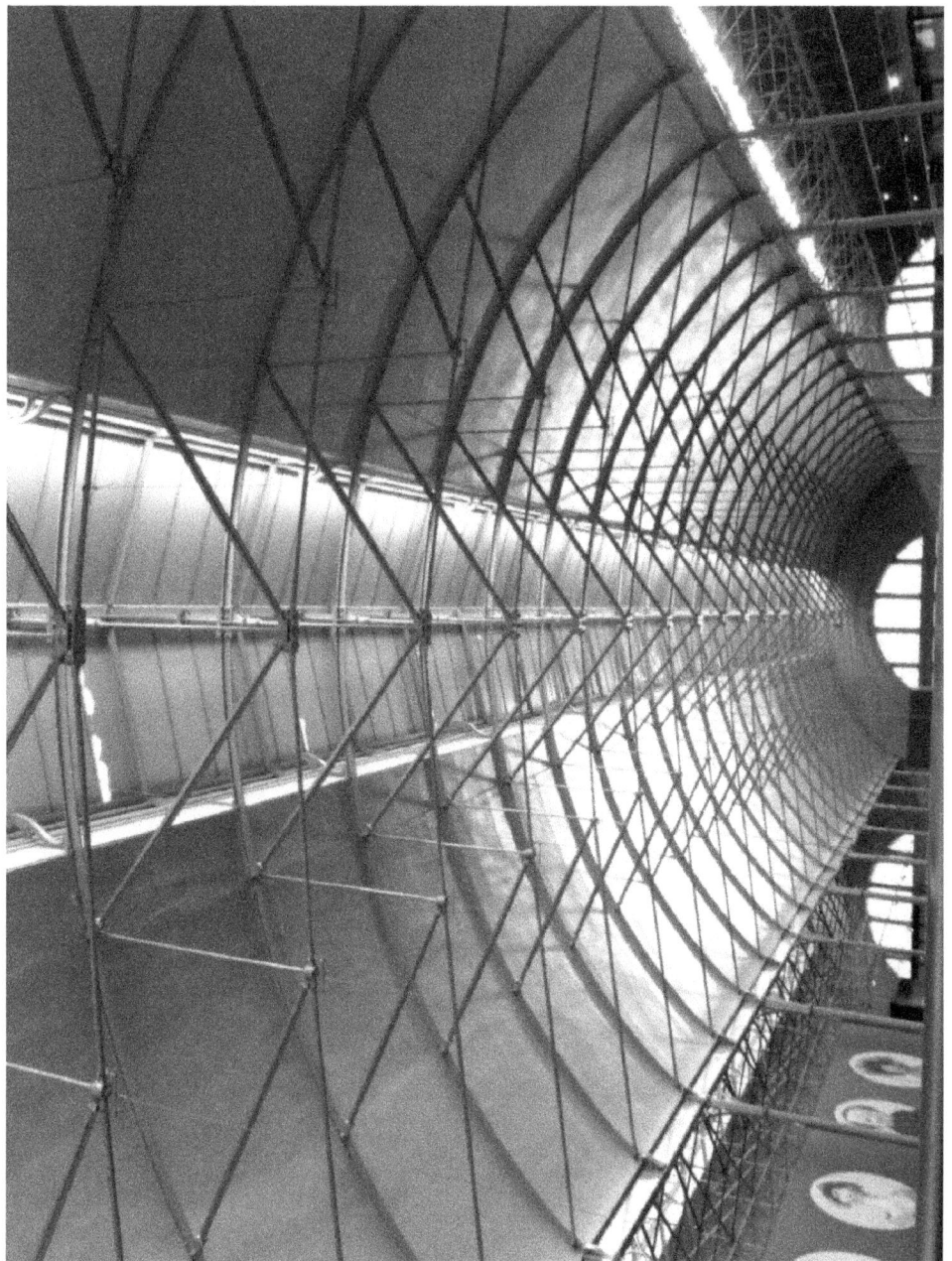

6.6.2015 - 17:00:28, Bethnal Green Children's Museum

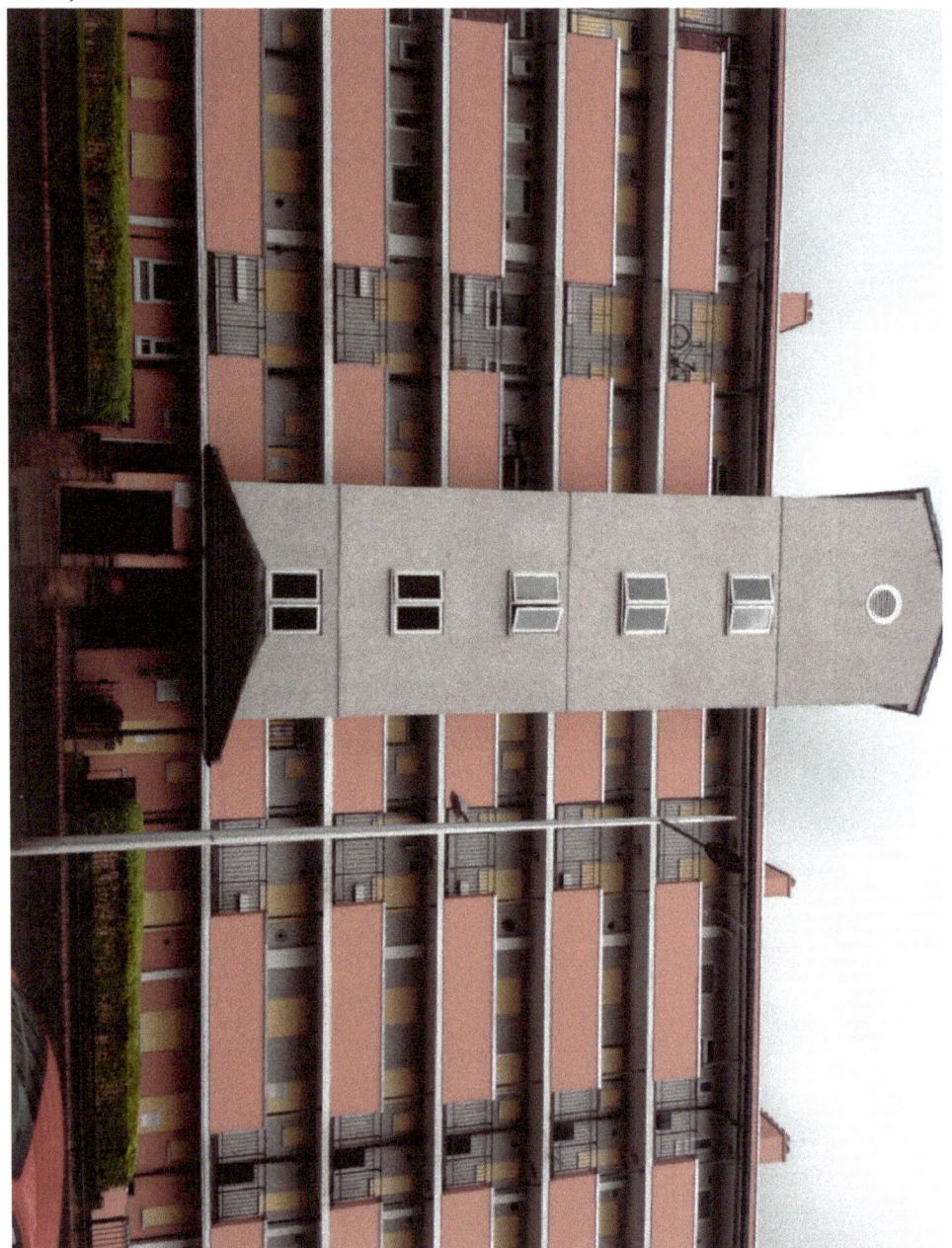

8.7.2015 - 12:58: St Pauls Way, Decant Building, Soon to be demolished

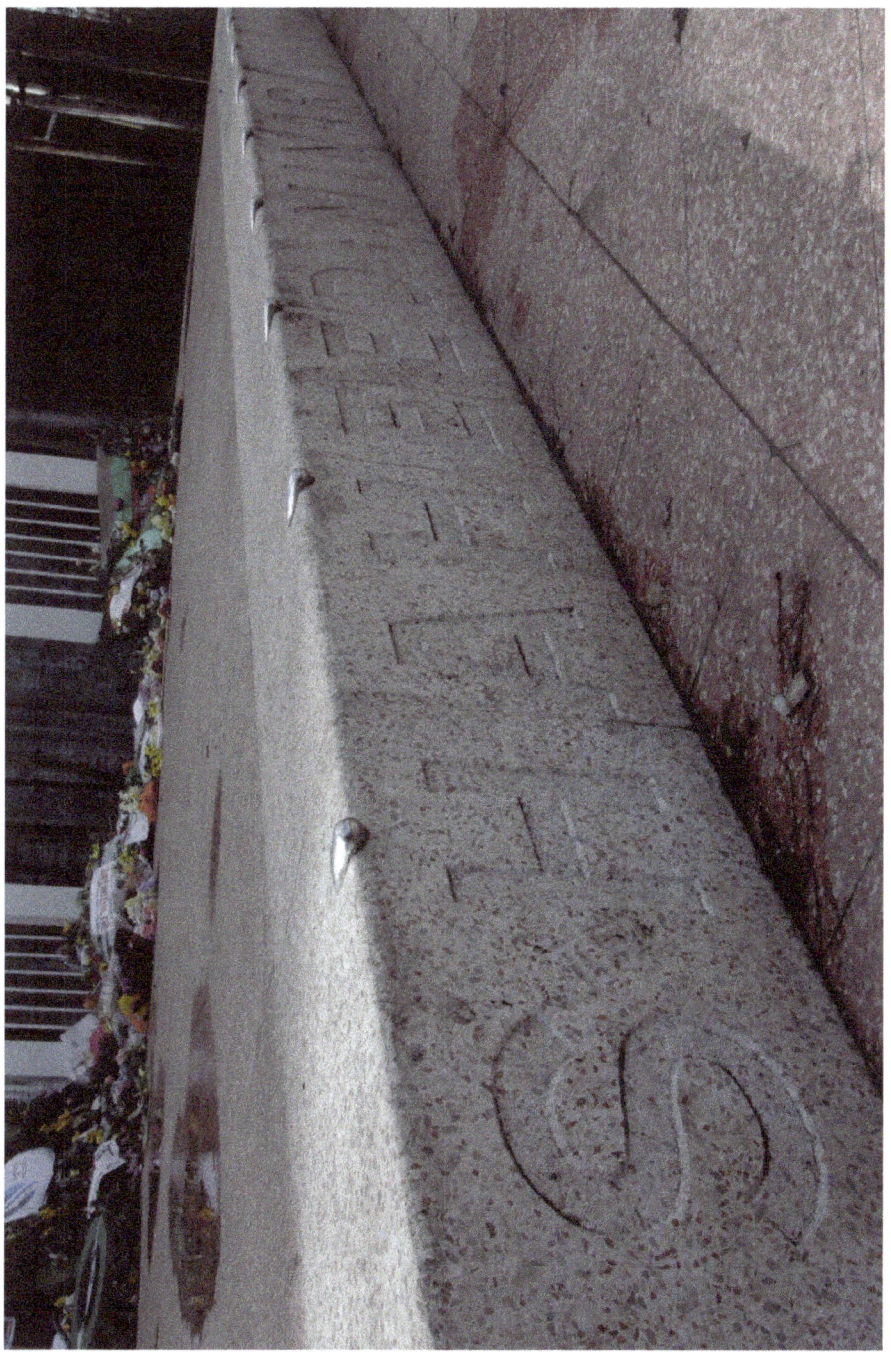

6.3.2004 - 22:32:16, Shihid Minar - Altab Ali Park, Whitechapel.

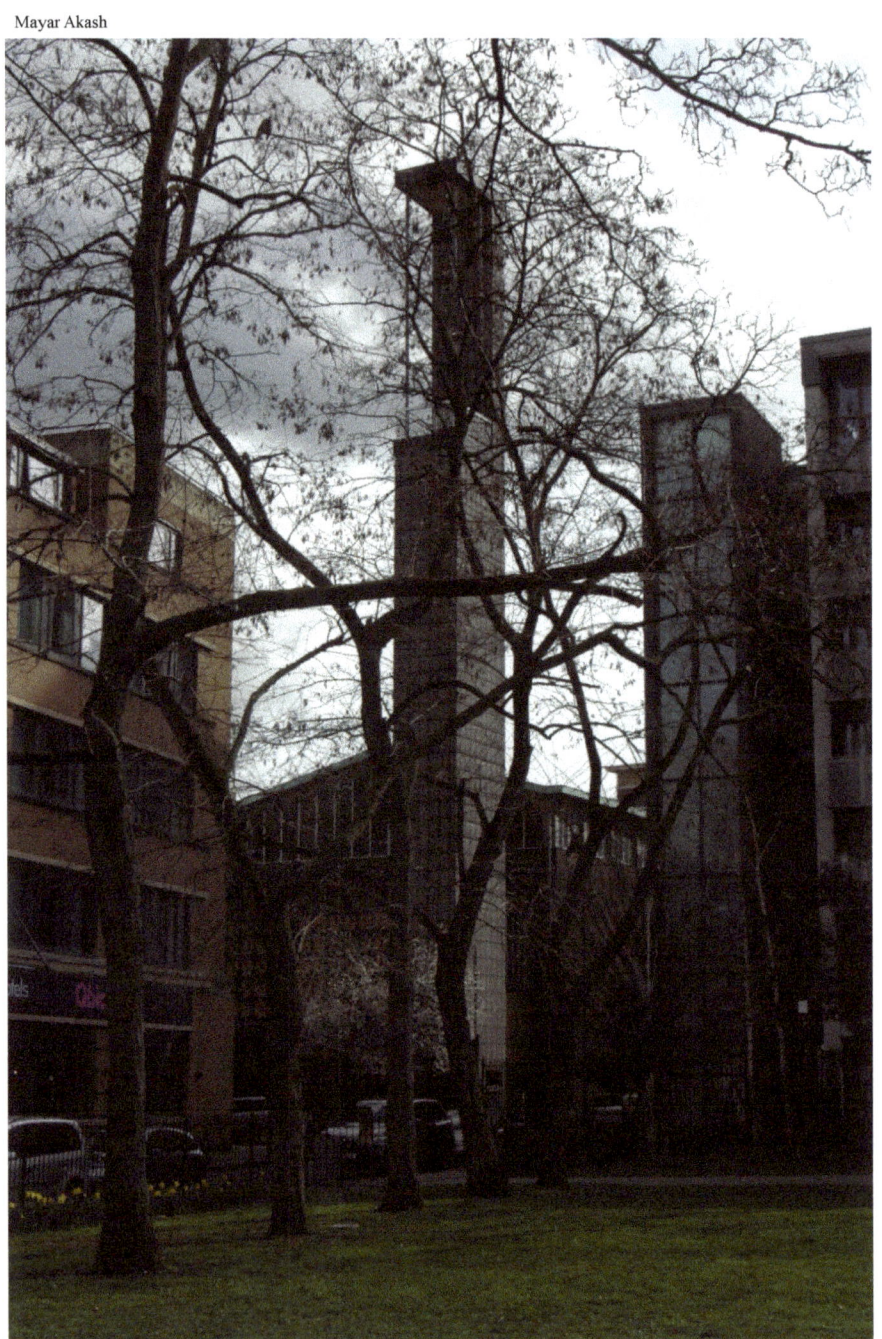

6.3.2004 - 10:25, Altab Ali Park

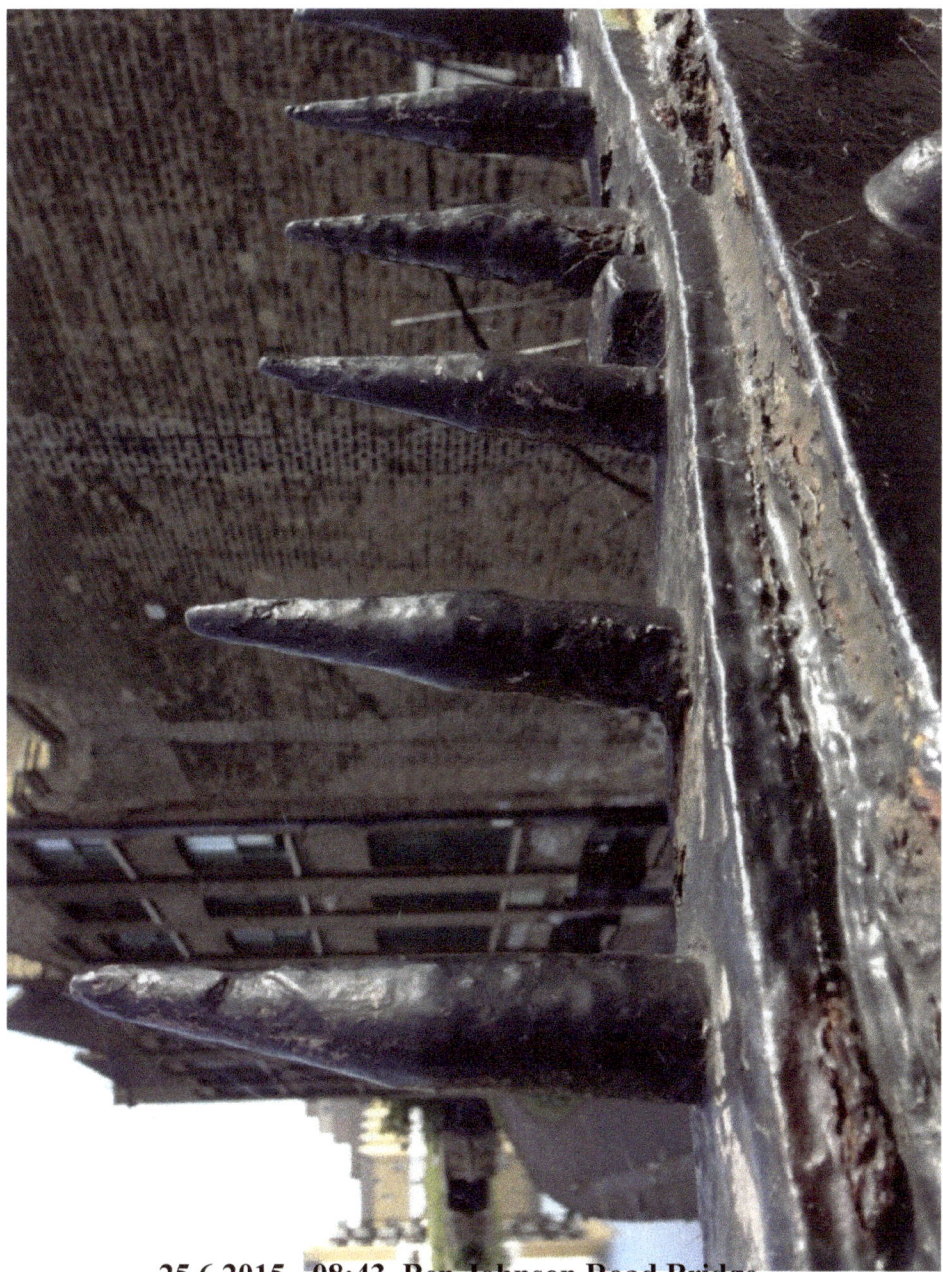

25.6.2015 - 08:43, Ben Johnson Road Bridge

On that day as I walked to work to Hailebury Centre, these spikes just caught my attention.

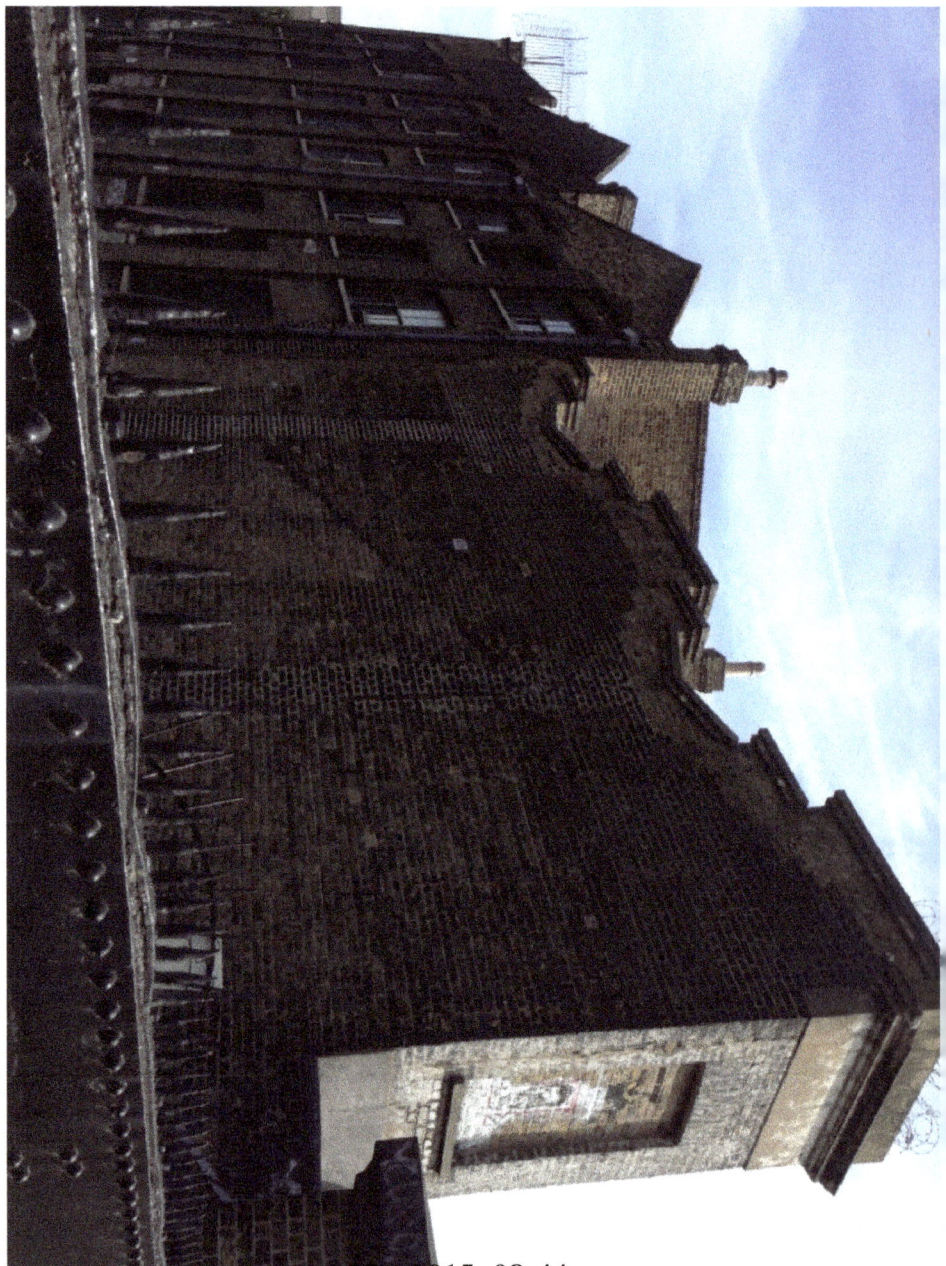

25.6.2015- 08:44
To me the spikes and the building were the preserved Victorian era, to hand.

East End Photos, Through Mayar's Eyes : **Tower Hamlets, Random One**

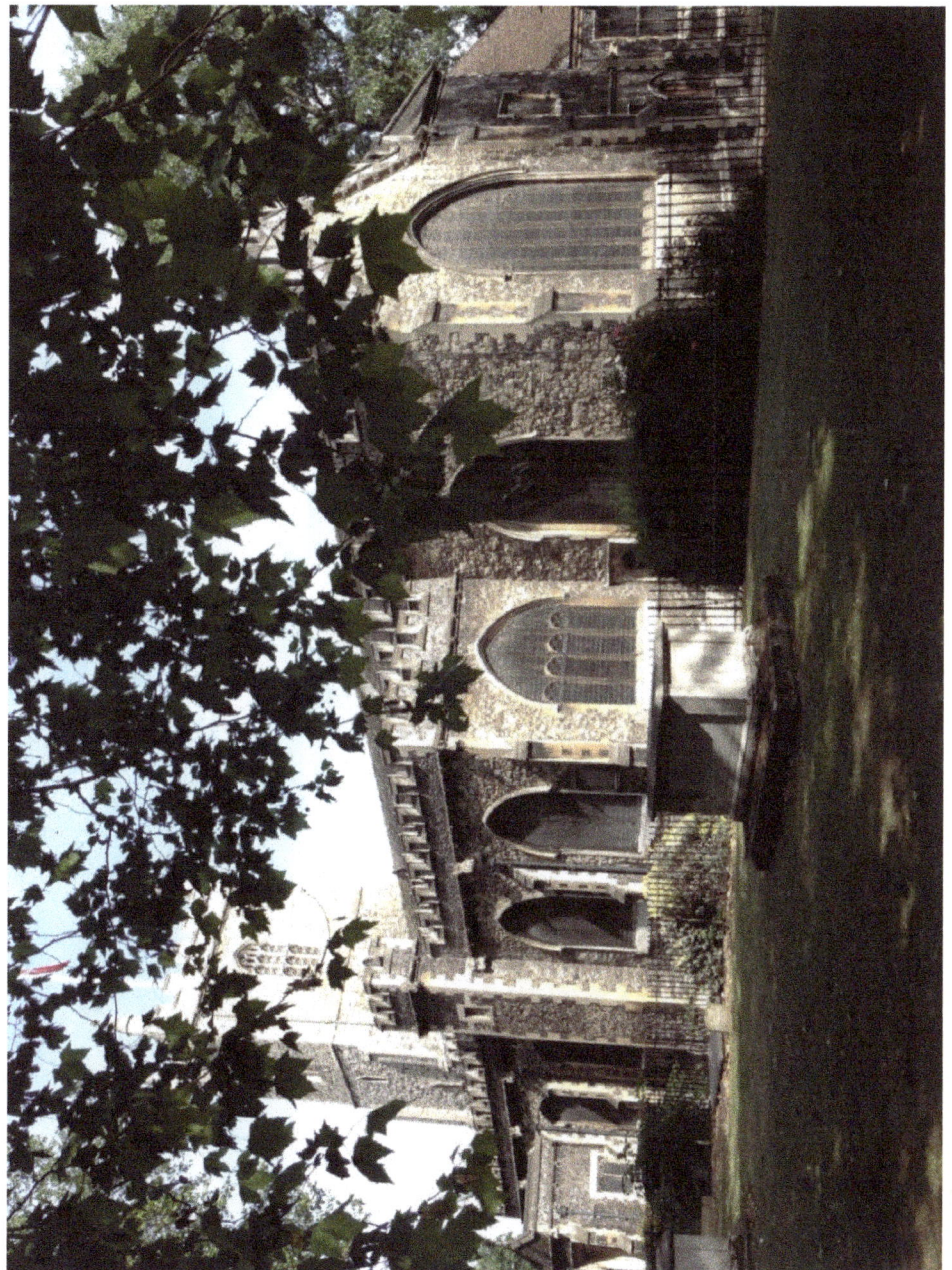

25.6.2015 - 08:52, St Dunstan's Church

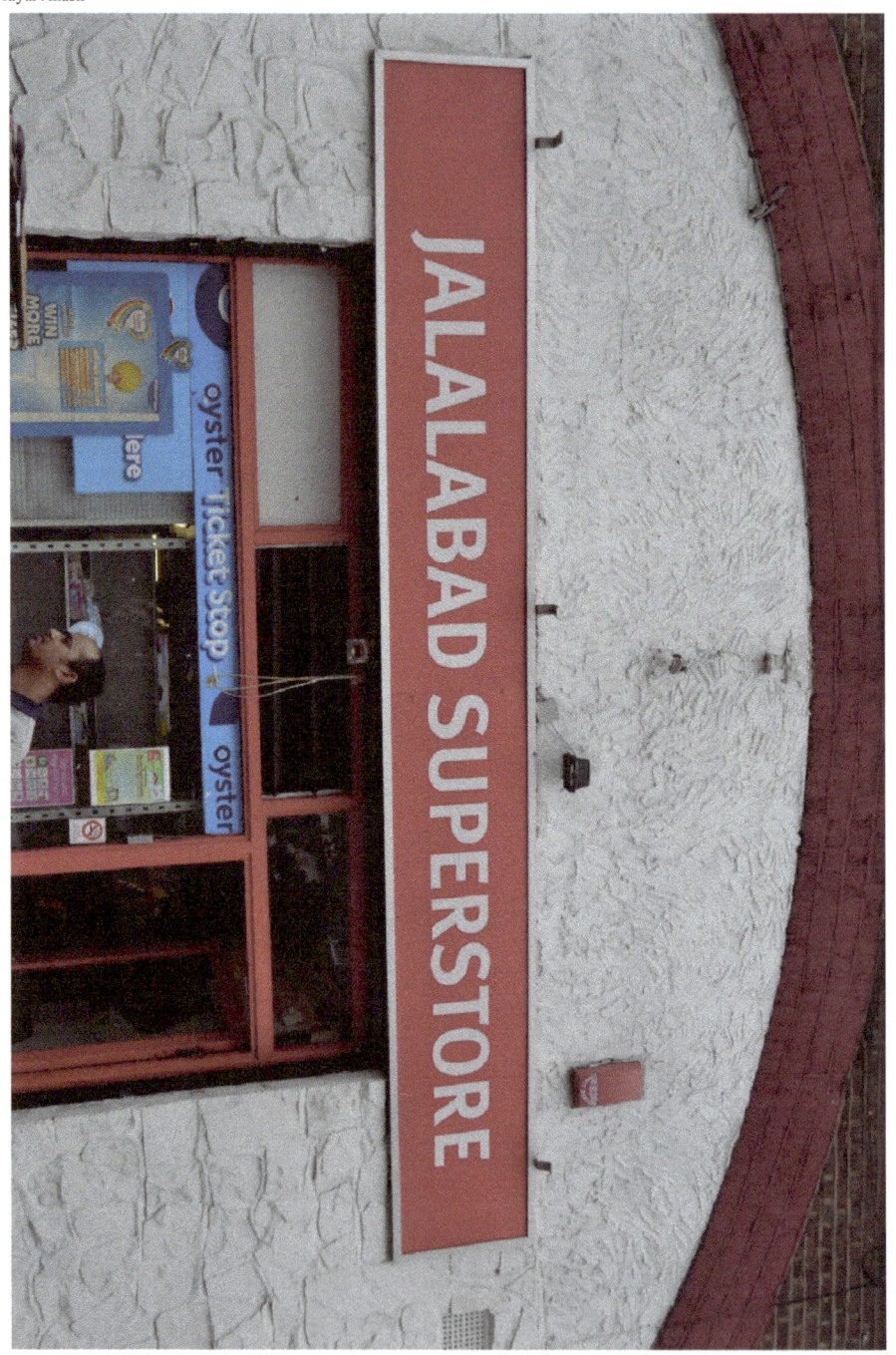

21.8.2013 - 13:53:38

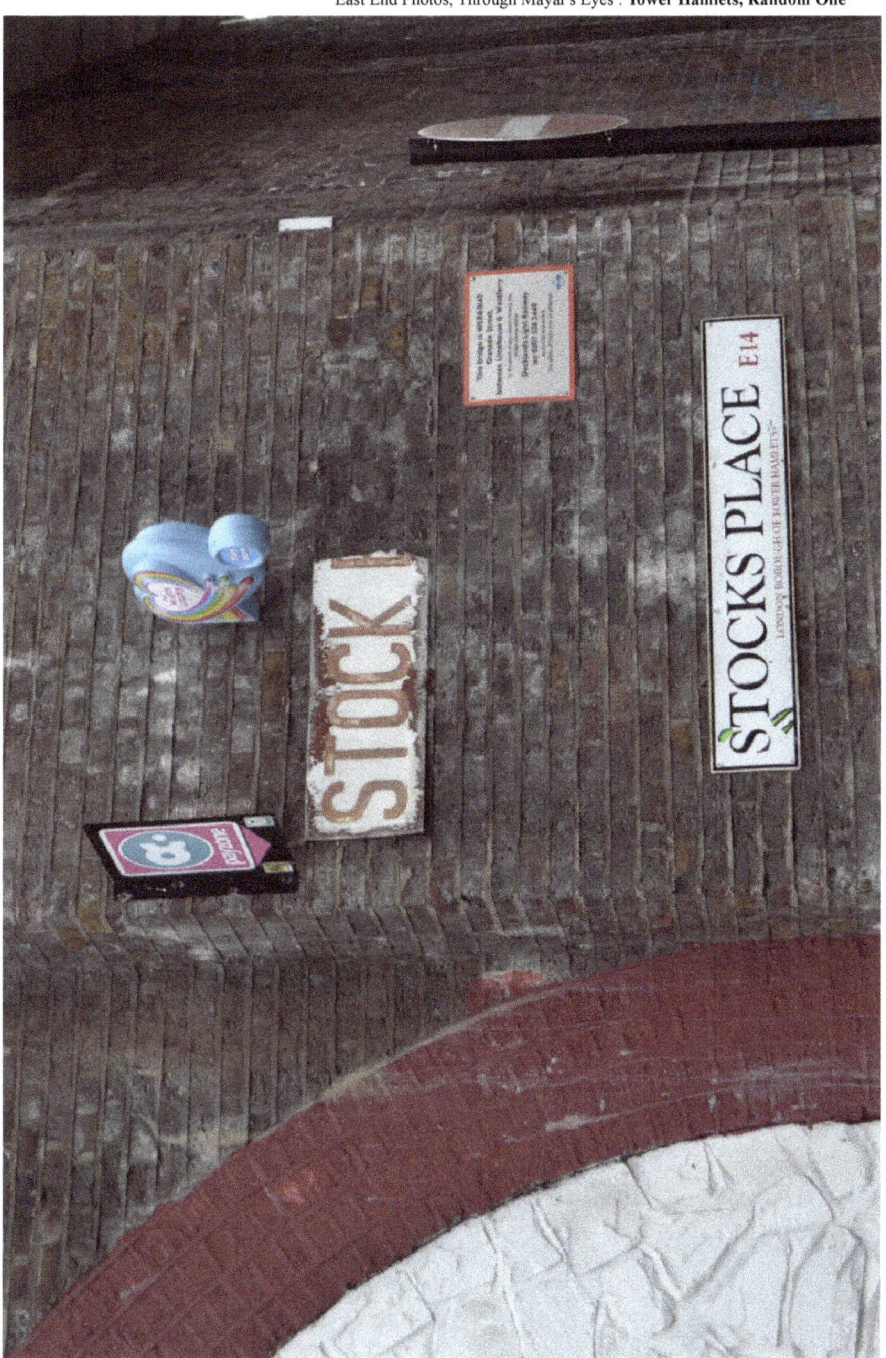

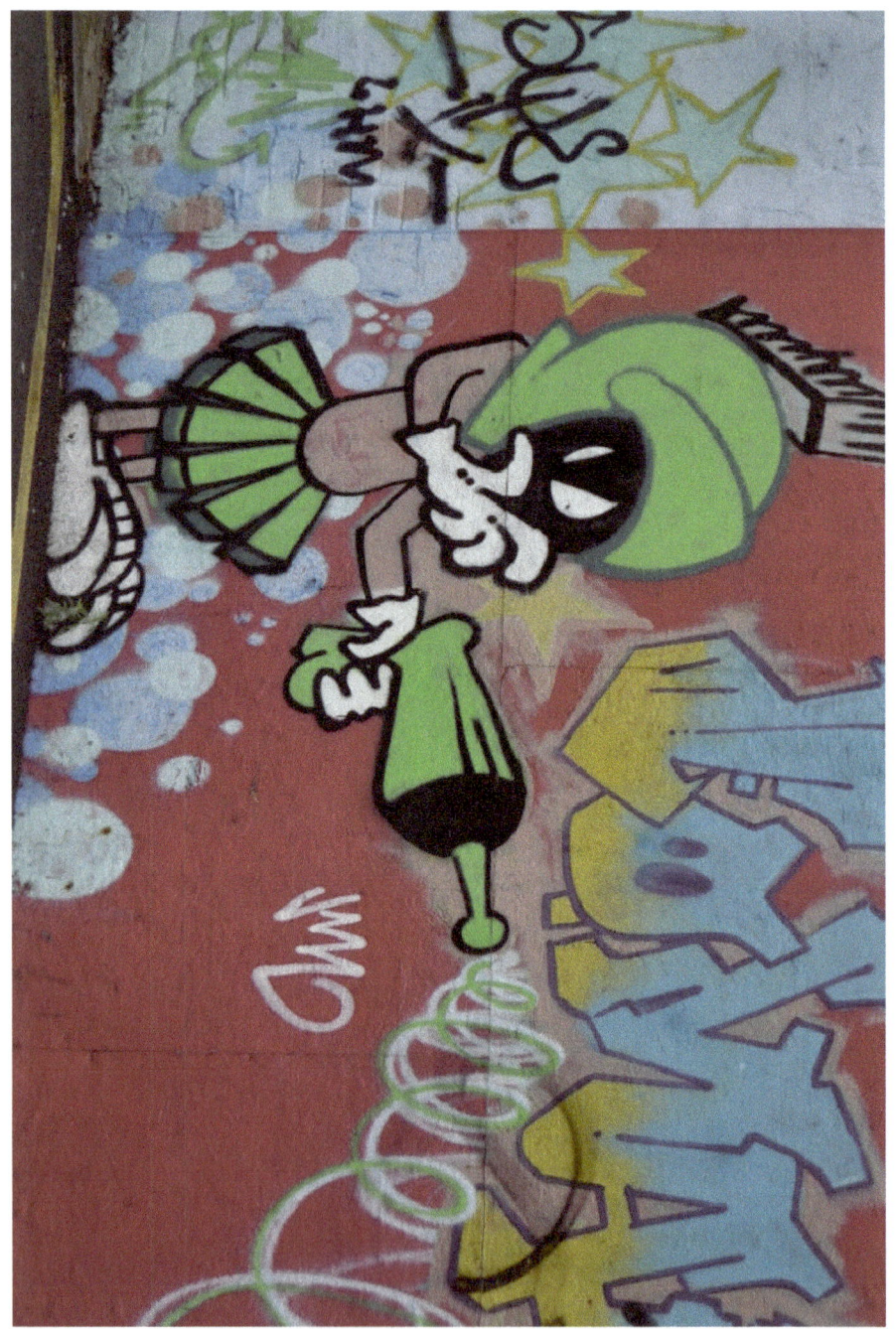

21.8.2013 - 11:19:22, Limehouse

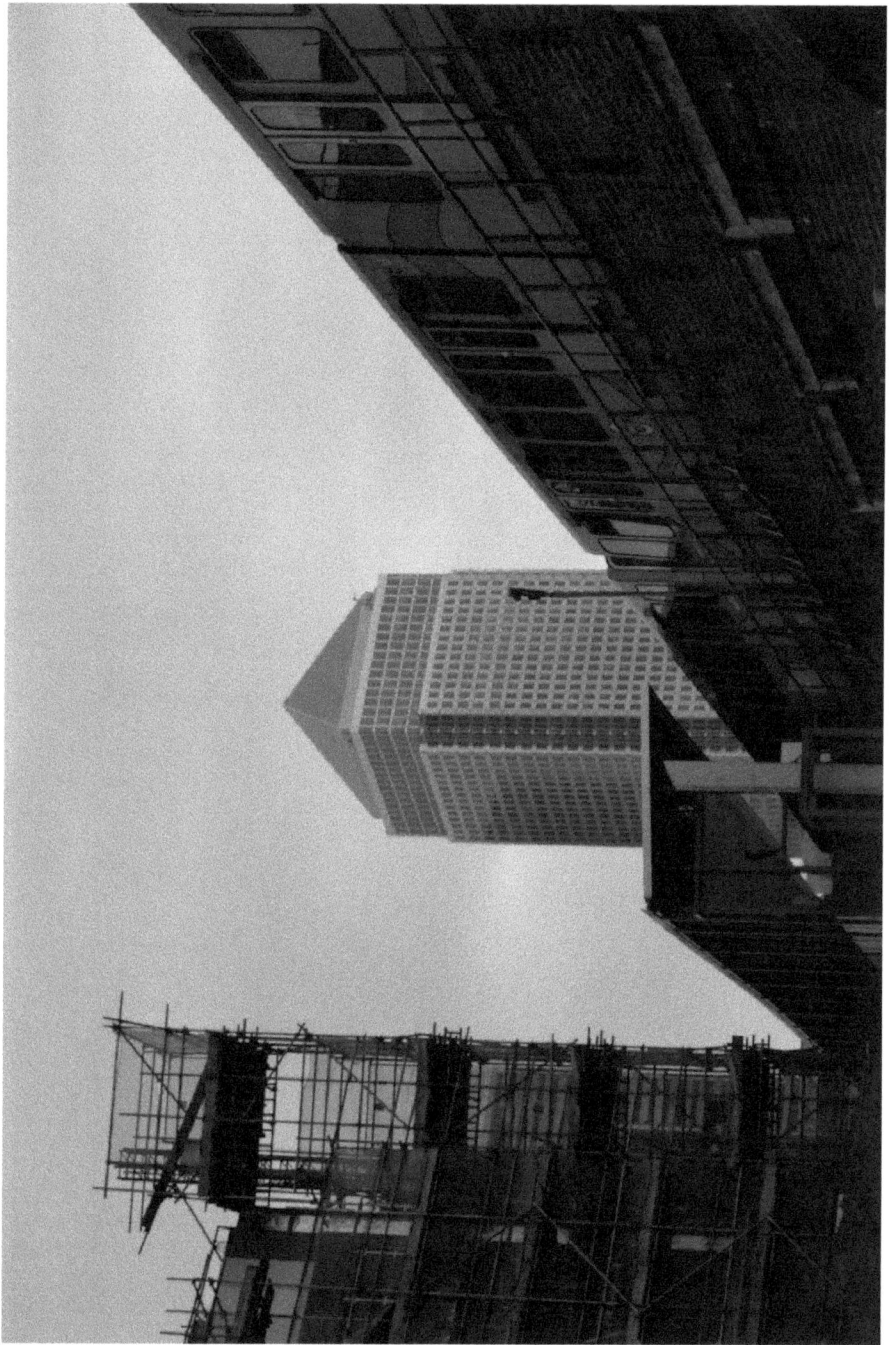

22.8.2013 - 12:48:10, Limehouse

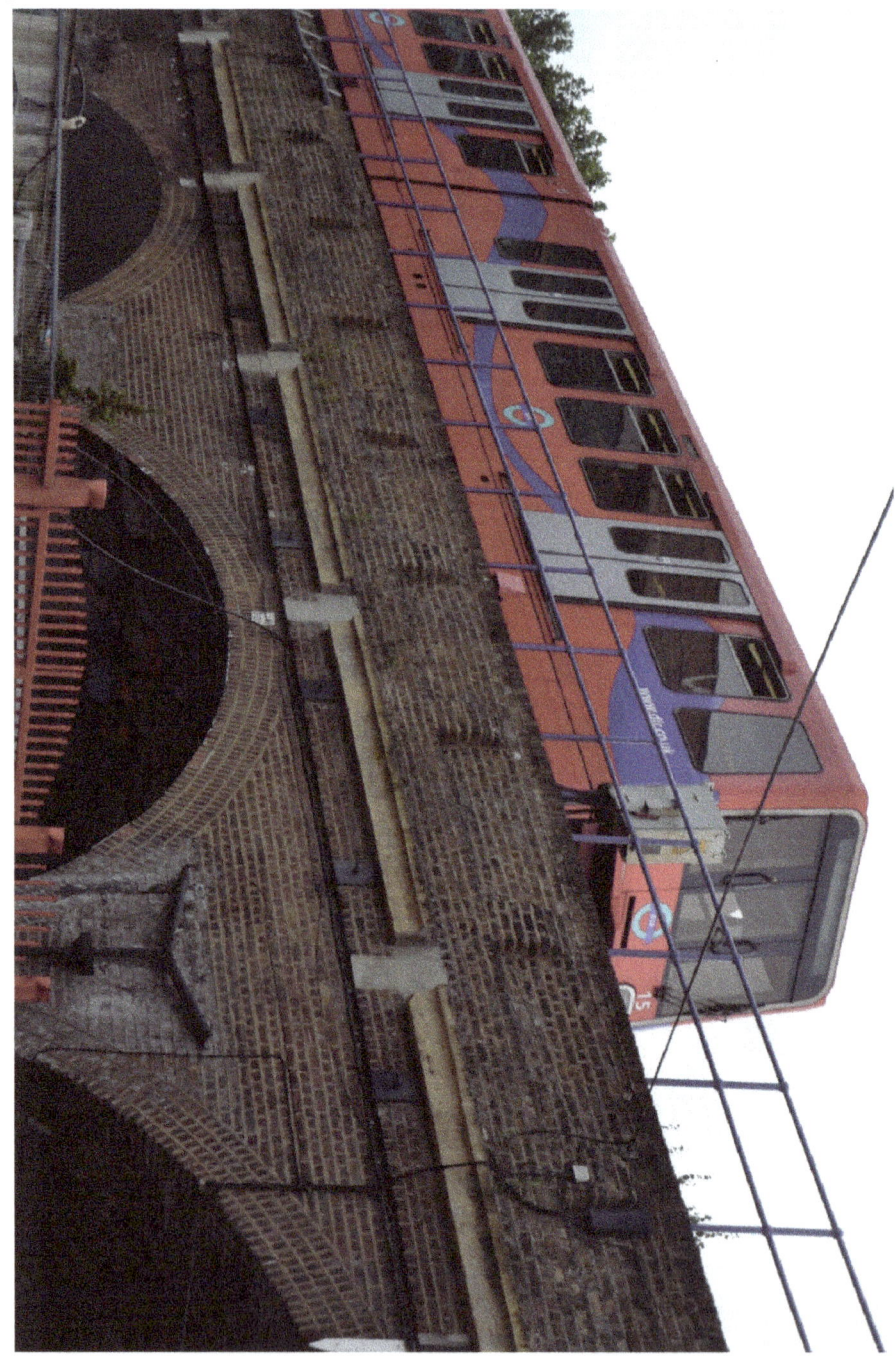

21.8.2013 - 12:22:40, DLR running through Limehouse

East End Photos, Through Mayar's Eyes : **Tower Hamlets, Random One**

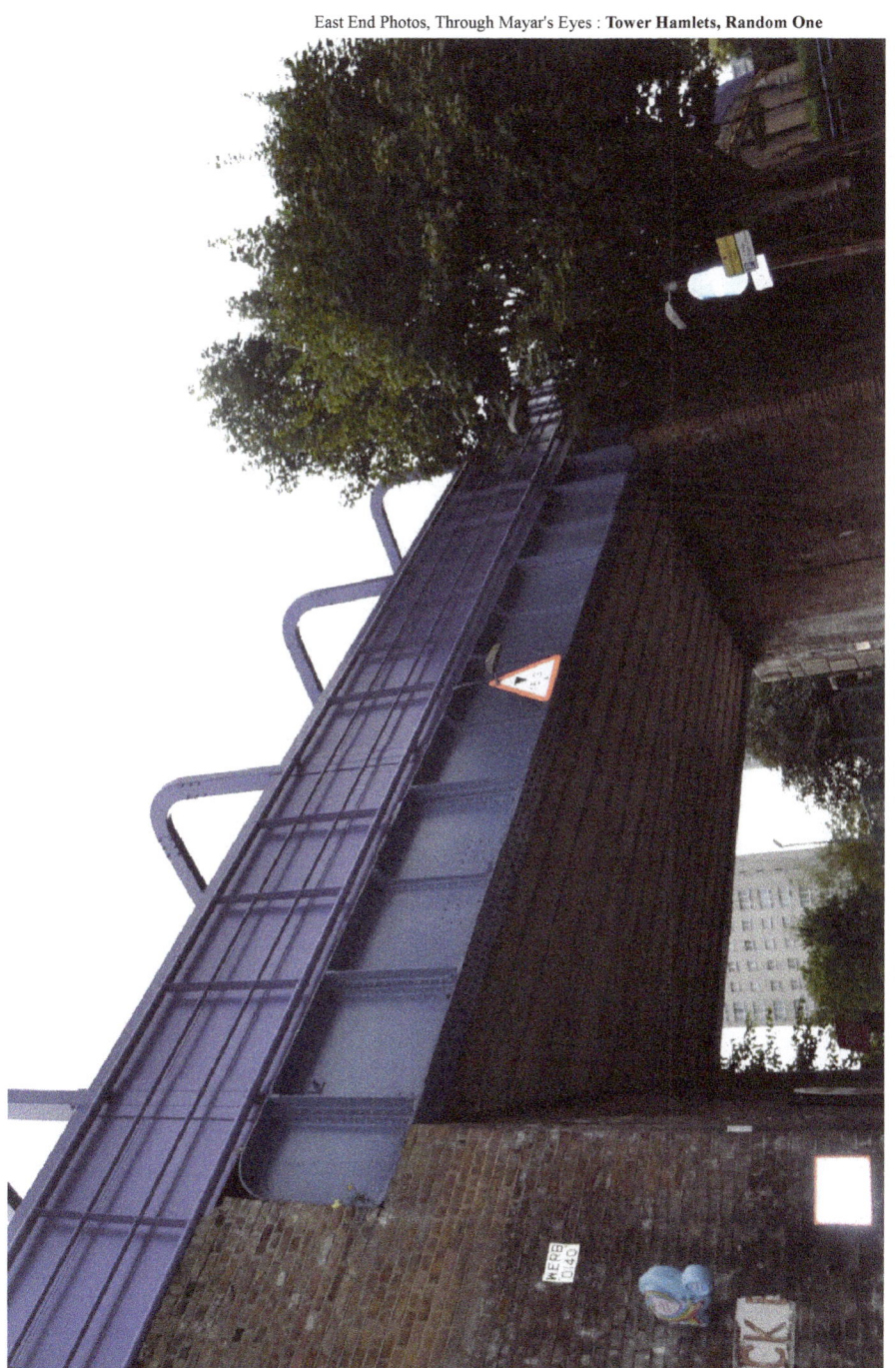

21.8.2013 - 12:25:56, Limehouse

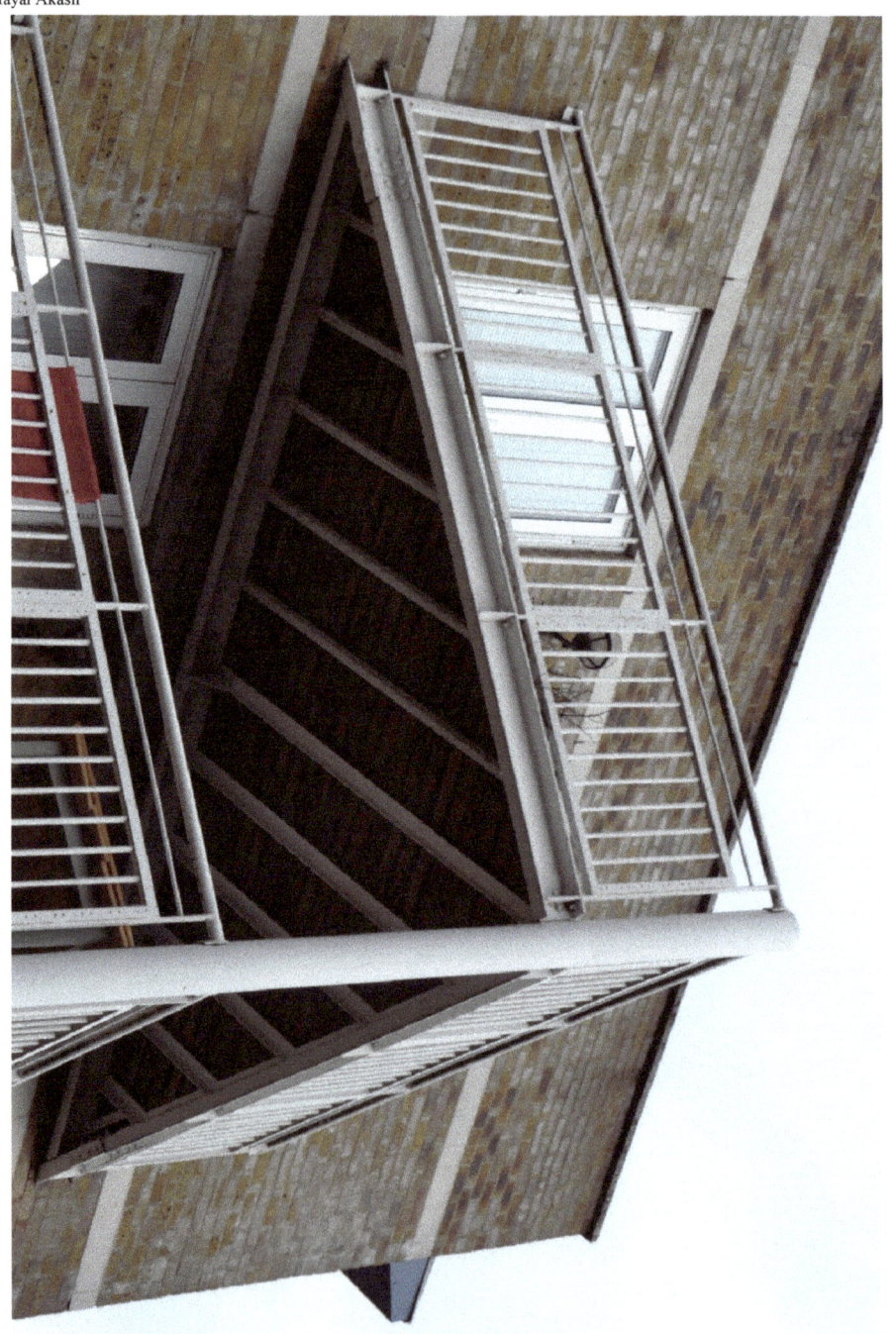

21.8.2013 - 13:54:34, Limehouse

East End Photos, Through Mayar's Eyes : **Tower Hamlets, Random One**

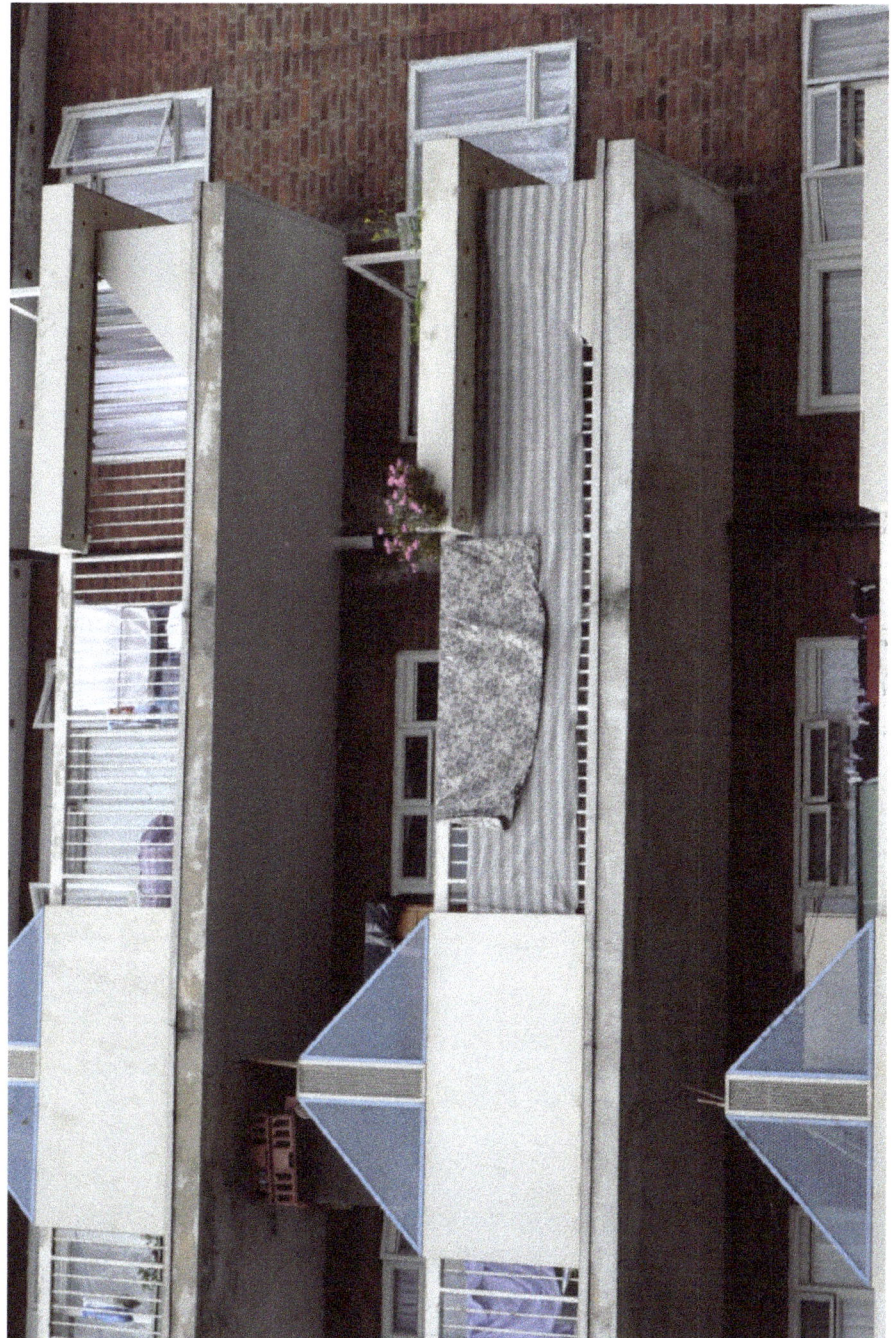

21.8.2013 - 13:55:04, Limehouse

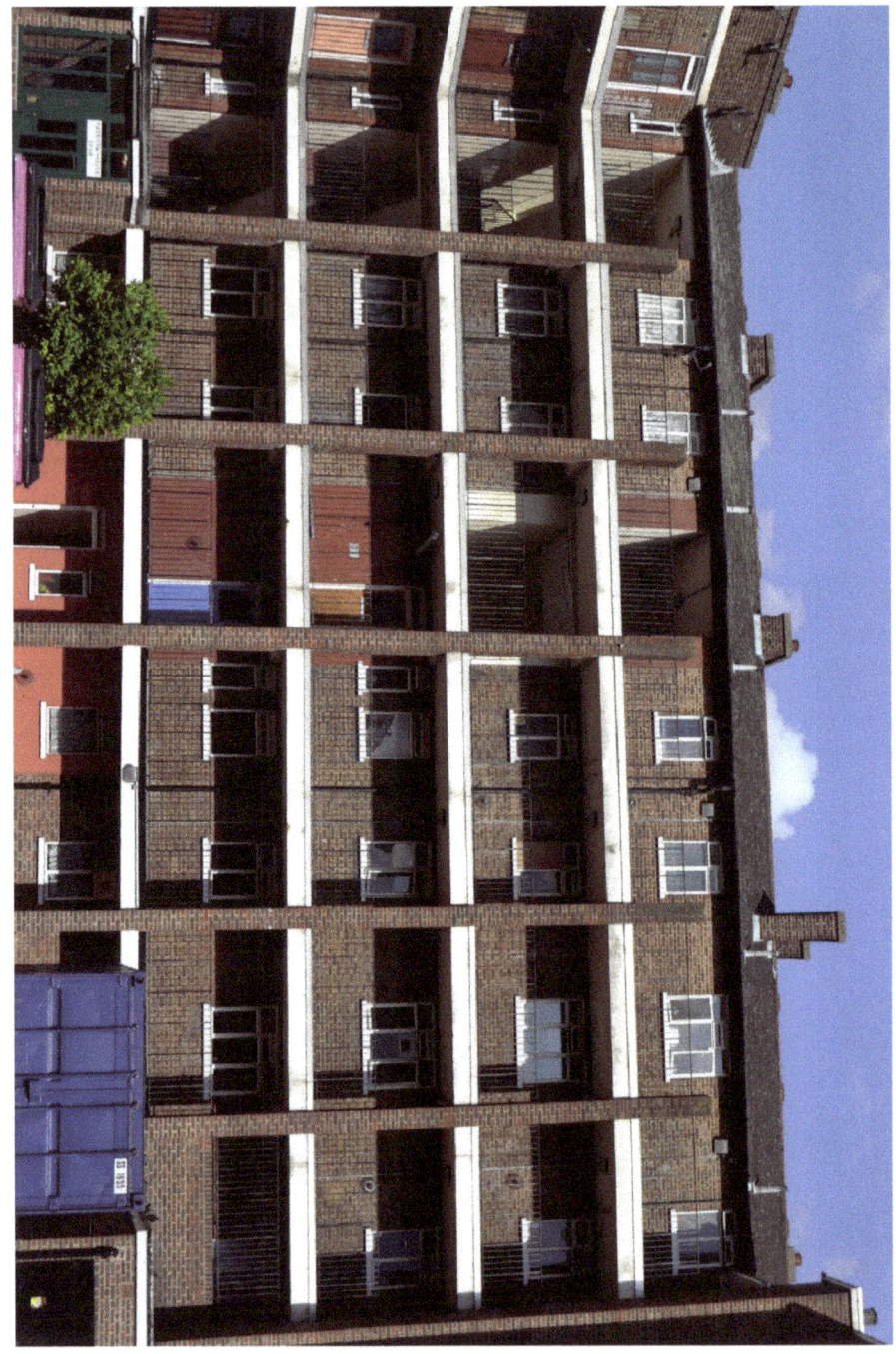

19.8.2013 - 12:30:36, Limehouse

East End Photos, Through Mayar's Eyes : **Tower Hamlets, Random One**

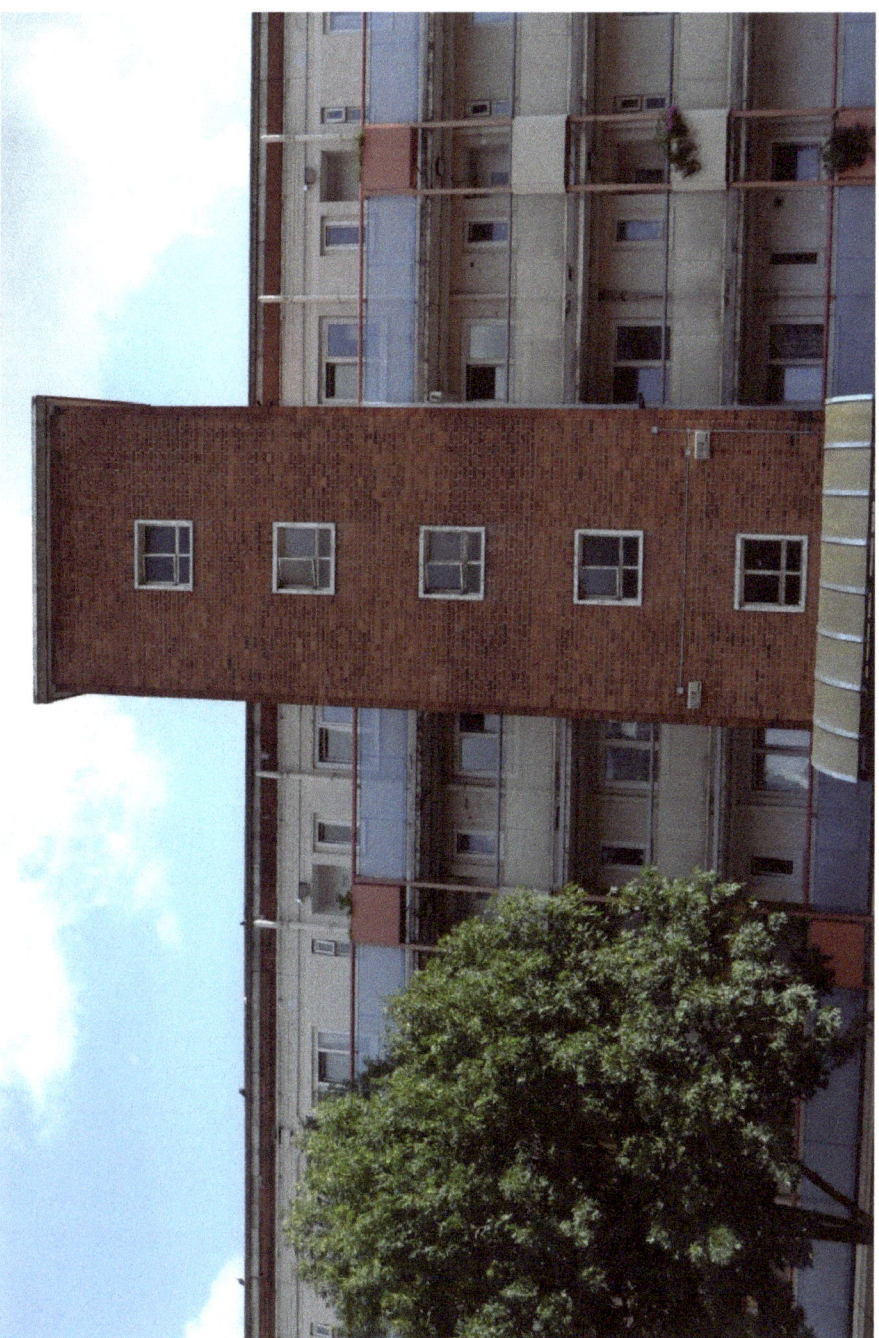

19.8.2013 - 12:34:10, Limehouse

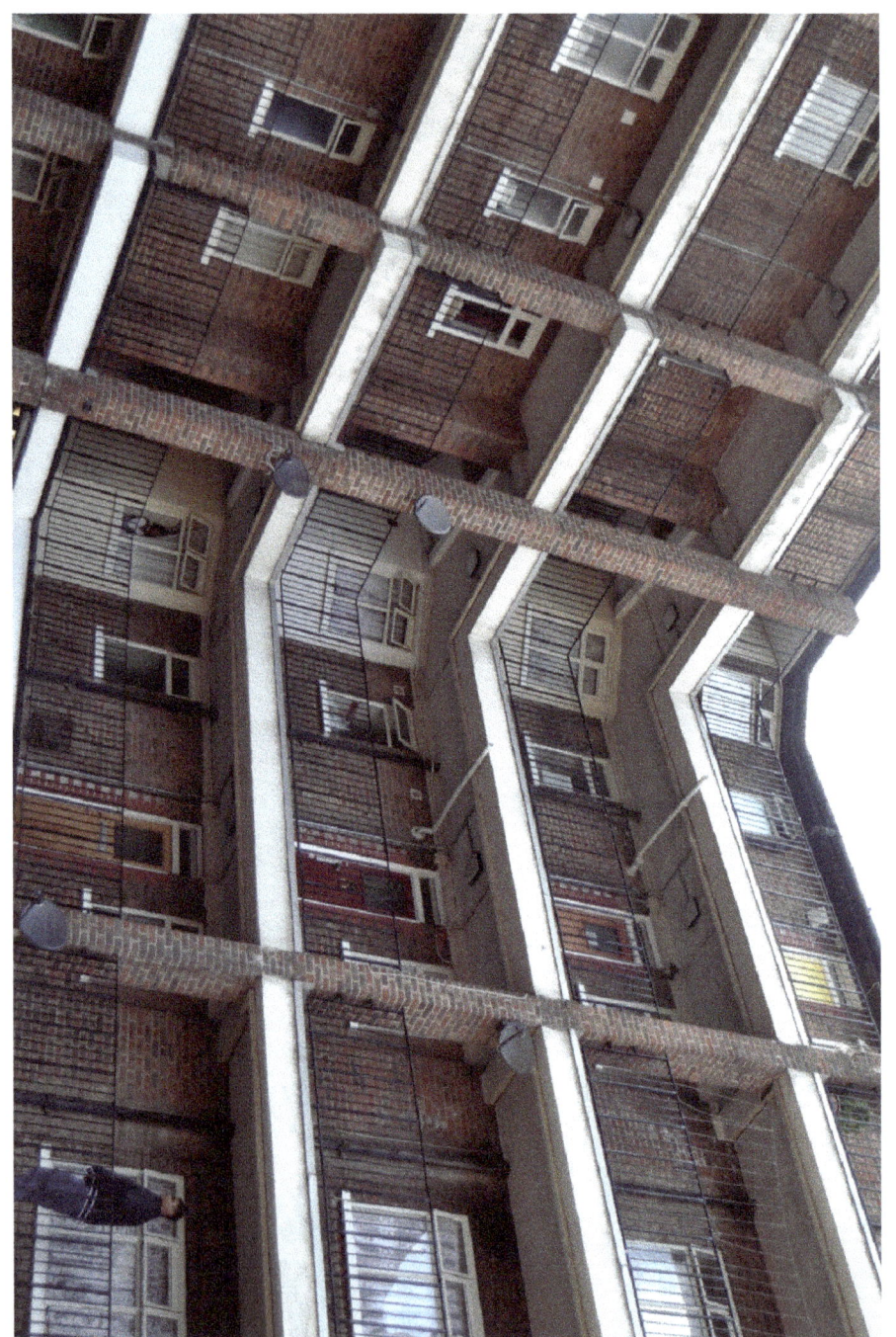

19.8.2013 - 12:39:34, Limehouse

East End Photos, Through Mayar's Eyes : **Tower Hamlets, Random One**

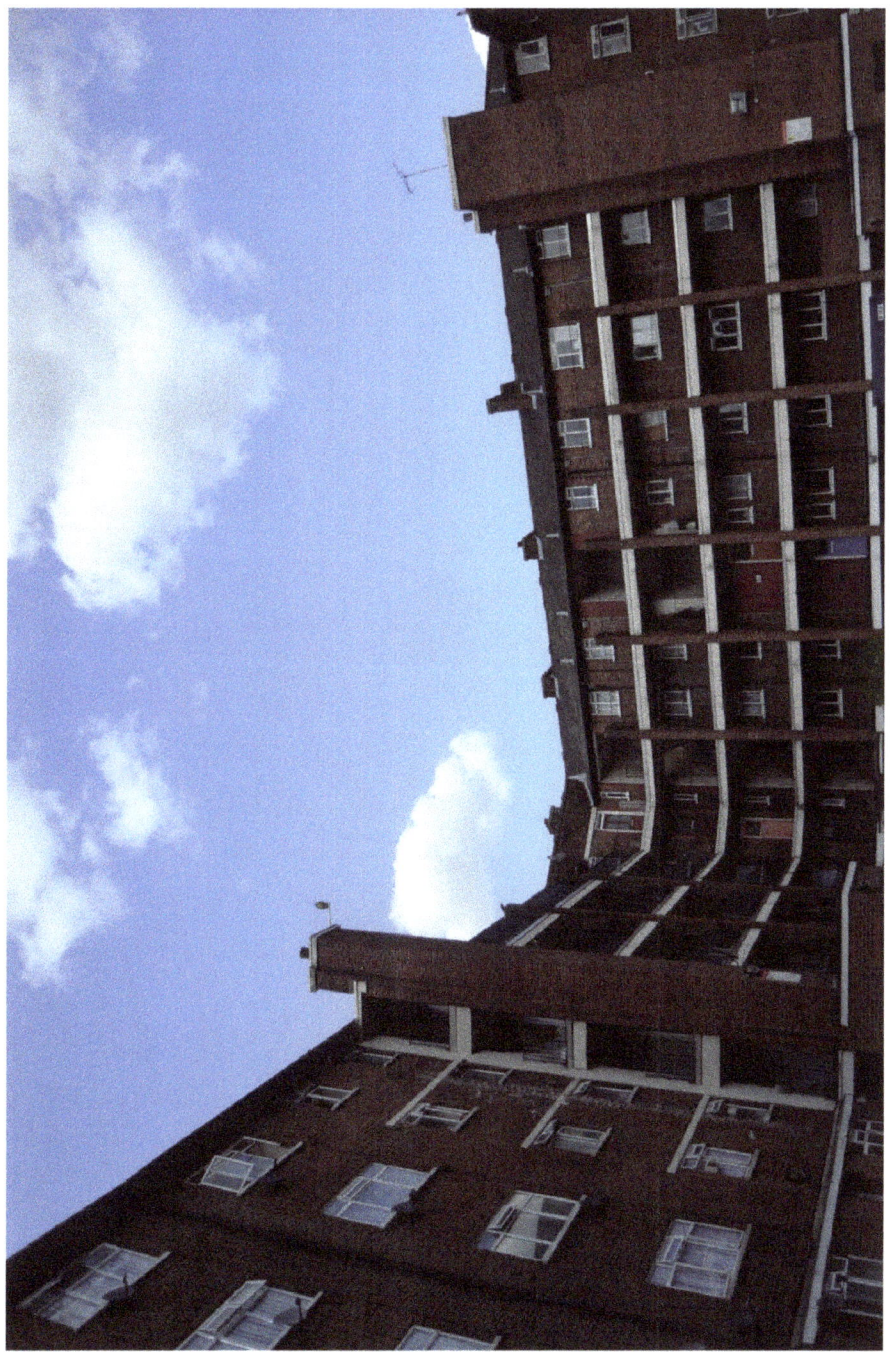

19.8.2013 - 13:04:16, Limehouse

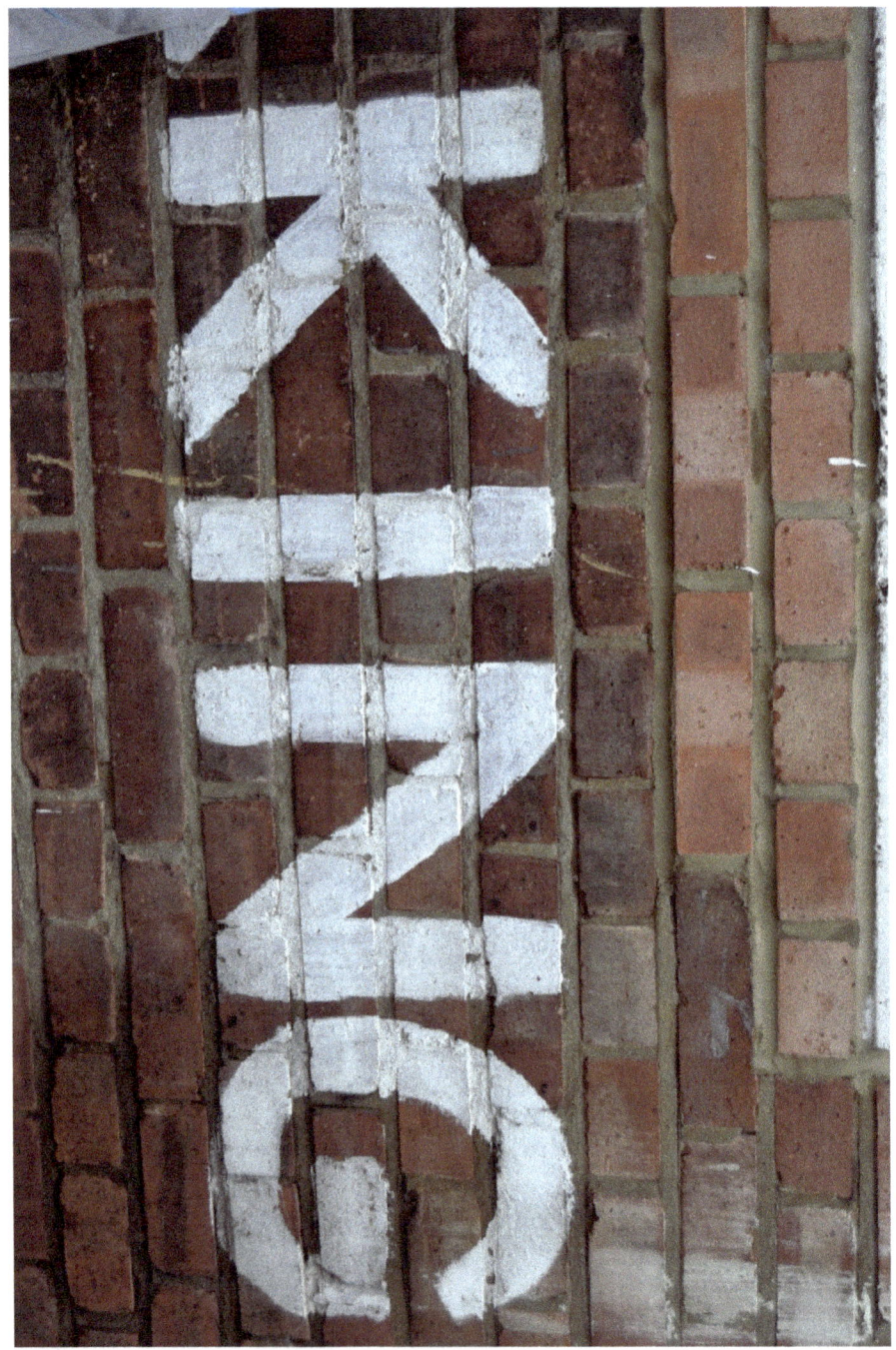

22.8.2013 - 12:52:34, Limehouse

www.ingramcontent.com/pod-product-compliance
Lightning Source LLC
Chambersburg PA
CBHW040521220526
45473CB00013B/2946